*The Mourners of Bayal*

# The Mourners of Bayal

Short Stories by
Gholam-Hossein Sa'edi

Translated by
Edris Ranji

Ibex Publishers,
Bethesda, Maryland

The Mourners of Bayal
Short Stories by Gholam-Hossein Sa'edi
Translated by Edris Ranji

ISBN 978-1-58814-149-1

Copyright © 2018 Edris Ranji

All rights reserved. No part of this book may be reproduced or retransmitted in any manner whatsoever except in the form of a review, without permission from the Publisher.

Manufactured in the United States of America

The paper used in this book meets the minimum requirements of the American National Standard for Information Services—Permanence of Paper for Printed Library Materials, ANSI Z39.48–1984

Ibex Publishers strives to create books which are complete and free of error. Please help us with future editions by reporting any errors or suggestions for improvement to the address below or: corrections@ibexpub.com

Ibex Publishers, Inc.
Post Office Box 30087
Bethesda, Maryland 20824
Telephone: 301–718–8188
www.ibexpublishers.com

Library of Congress Cataloging-in-Publication Data

Names: Sa'edi, Gholam-Hossein author. | Ranji, Edris, 1984-translator.
Title: Mourners of Bayal : short stories / by Gholam-Hossein Sa'edi ; translated by Edris Ranji.
Description: Bethesda, Maryland : Ibex Publishers, [2018]
Identifiers: LCCN 2017057206 | ISBN 9781588141491 (alk. paper)
Classification: LCC PK6561.S27 A6 2017 | DDC 891/.5533—dc23

*For my parents and my teachers,
with love and reverence*

# Stories

First Story ........................................................................ 9
Second Story .................................................................. 29
Third Story ..................................................................... 55
Fourth Story ................................................................... 90
Fifth Story .................................................................... 118
Sixth Story ................................................................... 143
Seventh Story ............................................................... 163
Eighth Story ................................................................. 182

# First Story

## 1

When the Headman came out of his house, Papakh, the Landlord's dog, started barking from the top of the garden wall and jumped into the alley. The other dogs that were sleeping on the low roofs of Bayal raised their heads and saw the Headman who, with his long stature, was walking in the moonlight; they put their heads on their forelegs and went to sleep again.

The Headman stopped and listened, the sound of a bell could be heard from outside the village. A faint, anxious sound, going away and coming close and whirling around the village. All the windows were dark. The Bayalers were asleep. And those who were awake were sitting in the darkness and looking at the moonlight.

Papakh came and stood beside the Headman and sniffed. The Headman was standing and listening, the sound of the bell went away. The Headman came to the side of the pool, Papakh following him. When they were beside the pool, a little window opened, a man's head came out of it.

The head moved in the darkness and said: "It's midnight Headman, where are you going?"

The Headman stopped. Papakh also stopped. Both of them looked at the head. The Headman said: "Ramazan's mother is sick, I'm taking her to the city."

Another window opened. Another man's head came out and said: "But she was well in the afternoon, wasn't she?"

"She was well in the afternoon. But she's not anymore." the Headman said, "She is no more well now. What if the old woman dies? What shall I do? Huh? What shall I do Islam? What shall I do with the boy?"

"How is she now?" Islam asked.

"She has rolled over and is lying down facing the Qibla[1]" the Headman said.

The first man bent and said to Islam: "He's going to take her to the city." Then he turned to the Headman and went on: "Isn't it better to wait till morning?"

"I'm afraid she won't make it till then." The Headman said, "I'm more worried about Ramazan. The old woman is consumed. I'm afraid the boy would do himself some harm out of sorrow, what shall I do to him? Huh? He is sitting beside his mother, weeping ceaselessly, weeping and crying."

"How do you take her to the city?" Islam asked.

"I'll take her to the roadside by your cart and I'll find a car," the Headman said.

Papakh saw that the Headman was talking. He sat on the edge of the pool and put his muzzle on his claws and closed his eyes. The Headman turned suddenly and looked back. Papakh raised his head too, and looked at the darkness.

"What is it?" Islam said.

"Do you hear?" The Headman said, "It's the sound of a bell, isn't it?"

Islam and the first man listened. But they didn't hear the bell.

"Headman, I'll go with you to take the cart back," Islam said.

He took his head in and lighted the lantern and put his cap on and came out by the window. The first man closed the window. His wife came and they stood behind the window together and looked at the Headman and Islam and Papakh's feet on which the lantern had cast light.

"What about your works?" Islam said.

---

[1] The direction that should be faced during Muslim prayers.

"I'll trust them to you" the Headman said, "My mind is wholly with Ramazan, I'm afraid his mother dies and the kid would do some harm to himself."

When they reached the other side of the pool, the light of the lantern was cast into the water. The fish came to the edge of the pool and looked at the men.

Papakh bent to see the fish, as soon as his eyes met the moon he turned back frightened and ran after the men.

"I'm taking Ramazan with me too," the Headman said, "If I don't take him…"

Their footsteps echoed in the alley. When the Bayalers saw the lantern they thought that Ramazan's mother had died. They rushed out of the windows; the old men, not able to get out of the houses, put their heads out of the roof-holes.

The cart was brought to the head of the alley as soon as it was ready. Everyone stood there silently. Islam and Mashdi Jabbar and Abbas and the Redhead took Ramazan's mother, who had been wrapped in a quilt, and put her in the cart and waited. Ramazan appeared, happy and cheerful, buttoning his vest. He came running, got on the cart and sat beside his mother.

Granny Khanoom and Granny Fatimah came to the cart carrying holy water. Granny Khanoom opened Ramazan's mother's mouth and Granny Fatimah poured a spoonful of holy water into the old woman's throat and the Holy Man who, with his large turban, was standing at the other side of the cart, prayed hurriedly.

Islam and the Headman sat on the driver's seat and lighted their pipes. The Bayalers accompanied the cart as far as the side of the pool and then stopped. Ramazan turned back and looked at them. The Bayalers were silently whispering prayers for them.

When they came out of the village, the road was light. Papakh ran after them for a hundred feet, returned suddenly, hid under the trees and stared at the cart. The bell could be heard from afar. When they moved for some distance the moon stooped more and more and grew large. Ramazan turned and looked back; Bayal had raised hands and was praying for them.

## 2

Islam and the Headman were sitting and had let the horse stroll by itself. Ramazan was lying down beside his mother and had put his arm under her head. Every once in a while he would bend, shake her and say: "Mom, mom, are you better?"

The old woman in whose bosom a vague pain was twisting and twinging, would softly say: "I'm better."

And Ramazan shined with happiness.

The Headman was at rest and satisfied and thought that the night was almost over. Suddenly Ramazan's mother's voice rose: "Raise my head, raise my head."

Ramazan raised his mother's head. Ramazan's mother looked at the desert and the darkness with eyes wide open.

"What do you want mom?" Ramazan said, "What do you want dear mom?"

"I want to know what on earth this is," Ramazan's mother said.

"What?" Ramazan said.

Islam and the Headman turned back and looked.

"This sound", Ramazan's mother said.

They stopped the cart. The bell could be heard from afar. The Headman nudged Islam and asked: "Do you hear?"

"It's the sound of a bell", Islam said, "The gypsies are passing behind the mountain. Their anklets jingle like this."

"No, it's not the gypsies", the Headman said, "It's not the time for them to appear yet."

"Oh yeah," Islam said, "It's the Poorussians, listen, they're passing at the bottom of the valley, taking with them the sheep they've stolen."

"The Poorussians never make a noise when walking, they come and go back like shadows" the Headman said.

"I know", Ramazan said, "It's Papakh coming, there it is."

And he pointed his finger at the darkness.

Ramazan's mother gaspingly said: "It's not Papakh... Papakh... hasn't ... got a bell."

The sound went away and was cut. The Headman raised the whip, the horse started moving again.

They went some distance again. Islam, who wanted to talk, said: "I hear a lot of these sounds, you know, I'm alone. I go on the roof at nights. I sit and listen. And I hear a lot of these sounds then."

Ramazan hooked his arms around his mother's neck and said: "Don't worry dear mom, Mashdi Islam has heard lots of these sounds, we're almost there, and you'll get well."

The old woman groaned and said: "I'm dying."

Ramazan started weeping and embraced his mother tightly and said: "I won't let you die, I won't let you mom."

Islam turned his head back and said: "Don't make a scene. We'll reach the roadside right now and we'll find a car."

Then he turned and asked the Headman: "How old is this Ramazan of you Headman?"

"He's finished twelve", the Headman said.

"Bravo, a man this old is crying, nothing's happened yet, why do you cry?" Islam said.

"I'm afraid my mom dies", Ramazan said.

"Your mom's not going to die, don't worry, but at the end she has to die, what are you going to do then?" Islam said, "Our mothers all have died. My mother, the Headman's mother, isn't it so Ramazan's mother?"

There was no answer.

"When you come back from the city, you must find him a wife Headman," Islam said, "why, the village is full of girls. And Mashdi Baba's daughter, plump, rosy and…"

He didn't finish what he was saying. The sound of the bell had come closer and closer again.

The four of them listened carefully. The Headman stopped the cart.

"Damn Abbas who has fastened the bells under the cart", Islam said.

He got off and went under the cart; he touched every corner but didn't find the bells.

When they started moving again, Islam said: "Never mind, when it is light, the bells will be found."

They went on and on. When it got light, the sound of the bells was cut and the road came into sight from afar.

## 3

By the roadside, Islam waited sitting on the cart, until a car was found for the travelers. Then he raised the whip and started moving toward Bayal as fast as the wind.

The Headman and Ramazan put the mother in the car and laid her down on rice sacks. Ramazan's mother was sicker. The pupils of her eyes could not be seen and she was panting.

The Headman was afraid that the old woman would die in the car. He wanted to take Ramazan away from his mother by any means. But Ramazan was holding his mother's shapeless, numb hands in his own and wouldn't draw aside. Sleep had filled his weary eyes and he could hardly hear; he could neither see his mother nor the dust of the road nor even hear the sound of the bell jingling around the car.

At noon, near a turn in the road, they stopped the car in a little shadow which had appeared from the notch of the mountain. The Headman laid the food on the sacks. Ramazan cut a piece of bread and filled it with wheat porridge, opened his mother's lips by force and poured the porridge on her teeth.

"She can't eat, let her alone", the Headman said.

The driver came and with his puffy eyes looked from the corner of the truck and asked: "What's wrong with her?"

"She's sick", the Headman said.

"Where are you taking her? Hospital?" the driver said.

"Yeah", the Headman said, "What else can we do?"

"But they don't attend to them in hospitals." The driver said, "You'd better let her die at rest in the village."

Ramazan and the Headman looked at each other. Mommy's breaths had become shorter. Her eyes were filled with dust. A bunch of green colored flies had perched around her lips.

"Wish we had brought a Quran", the Headman said.

"No, no, She's not going to die", Ramazan said, weeping.

"I know, I know", the Headman said.

"He is her son?" the driver said.

"Yeah, he's her son, and mine too" the Headman said while clearing the table.

The driver shook his head and said: "nowadays sons grieve less on their mothers' death. I was just like this boy. My mother died ten years ago, but I can't forget it."

Then he turned to Ramazan and said: "Don't worry, it's nothing, she's not going to die, I'll take you to a good hospital, there they'll attend to her and she'll stand up and walk again."

Ramazan sat up and swallowed his tears. The sunshine had just curved, and under their feet a huge valley with black rocks had opened its mouth. Ramazan said: "Look dad, do you hear? It's there!"

The Headman heard the sound of the bells. The driver said: "What are you talking about?"

"Don't you hear? Don't you hear the bells?" Ramazan said.

"Bells?" the driver said, "They're never heard around here, sometimes, crickets come to the edge of the road and gather there. But at night, and it's the middle of the noon now."

When the car moved, the sound of the crickets was cut.

## 4

When Islam entered Bayal, the people were gathered around the pool. He got off the cart and went toward the crowd and said: "They're gone."

Mashdi Baba who was sitting under the willow said: "No doubt the old woman dies, and the Headman is tough enough, nothing will happen to him and he'll come back to the village. But that kid, only God knows what'll happen to him."

From among the men Baba Ali said: "They must get an amulet for him and he'll be well."

Mashdi Jafar, Mashdi Safar's son, said: "It's nothing; he has already come of age, in one blink of the eye he'll forget about the mother and starts fancying other things."

"No, Mashdi Baba", Islam said, "We all know that Ramazan's mother dies. Then the headman takes his son's hand and comes back to the village. Ramazan will be restless for his mother, then I and the Headman will come to your house and suit the girl for him. When we get him a wife, he'll no more grieve for his mother."

The women who were gathered at the other side of the pool started whispering in each other's ears. Mashdi Baba's daughter, who had newly come back from a pilgrimage to *Nabi Agha*, hid herself behind the others.

"The Headman said so himself?" Mashdi Baba asked.

"No, I said and he agreed", Islam said, "As soon as they come back, I and the Headman will come to your house".

"Everything is in the hands of God" Mashdi Baba said.

Islam got on the cart and urged on the horse and went out of the village. The women sat down by each other. Mashdi Baba lighted his pipe and sank in thoughts and his daughter ran homeward, keeping close to the walls, and as soon as she arrived home, she stood in front of the mirror and put kohl on her eyes.

## 5

The janitor of the hospital opened the door. The Headman was sitting on the ground with his wife in his arms. As the door opened, Ramazan who was leaning against the door of the hospital, jumped in.

"Where do you think you're going?" the janitor asked angrily.

"My wife, this kid's mother, is dying" the Headman said.

Ramazan burst into tears. They were covered with dust from top to toe.

The janitor flung the door wide open. They entered the corridor which was dark and damp. They laid the old woman, whose eyes were wide open and was taking her last breaths, down on a bench.

"You'd better take her to another place. Such patients are not admitted in this hospital." The janitor said.

Ramazan cried louder.

"What other place?" the Headman said.

"You know, our hospital hasn't got a hearse or a car or anything like that. There are only several rooms and a doctor." The janitor said, "What would you do if she was not cured? How will you take her *there?*"

The Headman and Ramazan entreated him.

"All right," The janitor said.

They took Ramazan's mom and entered a large yard from the corridor and reached a second corridor and climbed the stairs up from the second corridor. Bandage and cotton balls stained with blood and mercurochrome were scattered all over the stairs.

A thin woman in a white dress was standing by the stairs with two little children and another child in her arms. As soon as she saw them she said: "Why are you bringing this corpse up here?"

"Let us bring her, she's still alive." The Headman said.

Ramazan cried loudly, and the woman approached and looked at the old woman's eyes and said: "Finished."

Ramazan's mother took a deep breath. "All right," the woman said, "bring her up here. You always bring patients here when nothing can be done for them."

They opened the door; a room appeared with a lantern hanging from the ceiling in which a candle was burning. There was also a dim lamp on the niche. Three empty beds, on which stained bandage and cotton balls were piled, were placed in the three corners of the room.

"You've lighted candles again?" The janitor said to the nurse.

"I'm afraid that I run out of oil and have to stay in darkness" The nurse said.

They put Ramazan's mom on a bed. Ramazan and the Headman drew back and sat down by the door.

"What are you sitting for? Get up and let's go call the doctor." The janitor said.

The Headman rose and went out with the janitor.

Ramazan rose and went to his mother and looked in her eyes which were fixed on the lantern, and he said to himself: "There it is, she's getting well, she's looking at the light."

"How long has she been sick?" the nurse asked.

"I don't know," Ramazan said, "we brought her to the roadside by Mashdi Islam's cart and brought her here by car from there."

The nurse's children were standing by the door and looking at the old woman and her son and the old woman's hands which were little by little hanging down from the edge of the bed.

## 6

The Headman and the janitor entered the corridor; they climbed up the stairs on the other corner of the corridor and reached a square vestibule with a round window installed in the middle of the wall, facing a large square. The janitor knocked on the door.

"Who is it, who on earth is it?" a man asked, coughing.

"A patient is here." The janitor said.

A thin man in torn cotton shoes and a white gown came out. He had crumpled a stethoscope and crammed it into his shirt pocket and was cracking and eating sunflower seeds. When he came out he stared at the Headman and said: "But he is not sick."

"The patient is down there, in Azar's room." The janitor said.

The doctor frowned and said: "Why did you take him there? I'm not in the mood to go to that filthy den every minute."

And he came downstairs. The Headman and the janitor followed him. They passed the corridor and the yard and the second corridor and climbed the stairs up. Azar who was standing at the door with the baby in her arms drew aside. The other two children who were sucking on a bone turned their heads and looked. Ramazan was afraid and went to the front of the window.

"You've brought these whelps to the hospital again? Take them out!" the doctor said to Azar.

Azar signaled. The children threw the bone down and went into the corridor. Azar herself went out too and stood behind the door and looked at the lantern from the crack in the door. The doctor went forward and put the quilt aside from over Ramazan's mother. He saw the familiar flies lined on the patient's face. The eyes were dried up; the dust of the last hour was floating in the old woman's pupils.

"And you two get out too." The doctor said to the Headman and his son.

Ramazan and the Headman and the janitor went out.

"She is very sick." The janitor said.

The Headman drew the janitor to a corner and said: "My son will kill himself if the old woman dies. I know it, what shall I do with him?"

"You believe so?" the janitor said.

"Yeah," the Headman said, "he hasn't moved from his mother's side for ten days. I know that the old woman's dead. For the sake of God, do something not to let the boy figure it out."

"All right," The janitor said.

When the room was empty, the doctor uncovered the patient's bosom. The old woman's green body was becoming cold.

The doctor put the stethoscope on the patient's heart. It had stopped beating. But a faint and unintelligible sound could be heard. The doctor turned away angrily and opened the door and said to Azar: "How many times should I tell you not to give the kids toys when I'm visiting patients?"

Azar showed him the children who were sitting on the stairs, waiting noiselessly. The doctor returned and put the stethoscope on the heart again. The sound of the bell went away little by little and...

It died out at the end of the desert.

## 7

Mashdi Baba's daughter put the kohl on her eyes, came on the roof and sat down. None of the Bayalers were out, Papakh was on the Headman's house wall and had put his head on his forelegs and was asleep.

Mashdi Baba was lying in the room; he was playing with his Henna-dyed beard and looking at his daughter's red breeches from the roof-hole.

Islam entered the village riding the cart and went to the side of the pool, he filled the bucket and held it before the horse's mouth. The horse drank. Islam's black goat came out by the window and went to the side of the cart and started licking the crumpled grass sticking to its wheels. The night was coming. Everyone was waiting. They would put their heads out of the windows and listen.

The road was quiet and dark.

Mashdi Baba's daughter was sadly sitting on the ledge of the roof.

## 8

Ramazan was happily eating bread and yogurt in the janitor's room. His mother was silent, not groaning. They had covered her with a sheet. The janitor had told him that his mother had to have an operation to get well again and to do that, it was appointed to take her to another hospital tomorrow morning.

The three of them were staying in the janitor's room. When Ramazan finished his dinner, he lied down and went to sleep. But the janitor and the Headman were talking softly until the midnight. The janitor was teaching the Headman the rules.

They put the lamp out and laid themselves down. Outside, the wind was blowing and rubbing the bough of the almond tree on the window panes.

The janitor and the Headman woke up in the morning. They went out of the room on tiptoe and brought Ramazan's mother down from Azar's room and laid her on the bench in the corridor. They opened the door and went to the street and they were waiting for a car to take the corpse to the cemetery when Ramazan woke up and came out.

"We want to send your mom to another hospital to have an operation." The janitor said.

"I'll go with her." Ramazan said.

"They won't let you in there." The janitor said.

"I'll come back if they didn't let me in there." Ramazan said.

A black car appeared. The janitor haggled with the driver and the Headman took Ramazan's mother in the car and sat. And Ramazan sat beside the Headman.

The car started moving, the janitor watched them. When they were at the head of the street, the sun rose and the driver turned his head back and said: "Why have you crumpled the patient like that? You don't mean that… huh? You don't mean that…?"

"We get off at the head of *the* alley. The violet-bed alley." The Headman said.

The driver said nothing; he drove on and on and stopped at an empty little square. They got off. There was a long alley before them which was full of dust. A black stone was fallen in the corner of the alley. There was a little banner installed on the stone, with a copper palm.

"You sit down right here, I'll take your mom and come back." The Headman said.

"I'll come with you; I want to see my mom." Ramazan said.

He reached for the corpse's hand in the quilt.

"Don't touch her," the Headman said, "If she wakes up, she'll never get well. You stay right here. They won't let us in if you come. What are we supposed to do then?"

Ramazan sat on the stone. He put the bundle of yogurt and bread on his lap. The Headman entered the alley, carrying Ramazan's mother on his shoulders. Mom's blackened feet had fallen out from under the quilt, her long loose toes made grooves on the soft soil of the alley.

Ramazan was looking at the grooves which lengthened as his father moved forward. The sun was hot and blazing. A stinky wind was blowing and shaking the banner over Ramazan's head. Sound of wheels and bells echoed in the alley. Ramazan drew aside. A black coach appeared which was being drawn by two healthy horses. Little bells were hanging from the cords on the sides of the coach. The coach entered the small square and stopped. The horses refreshed and strode toward the street and made the bells jingle.

The coach was getting out of the square, from under its curtain a big, green candle fell on the ground. The wheels passed by it.

## 9

Islam and Mashdi Baba were on the cart. Mashdi Baba's daughter was sitting in the end of the cart with kohl-dyed eyes. They had come to the roadside and were waiting.

"I don't think they'll be late." Islam said, "The old woman was so sick. When they were putting her in the car she was giving up the ghost. They'll be here any moment."

"The Headman is a pious man, he won't return till he has buried the corpse." Mashdi Baba said.

There was not a single soul on the road. Mashdi Baba's daughter was looking in the direction of the city with waiting eyes.

Islam turned suddenly and looked at the bed of the road. Two big mice were approaching slowly. Islam got off the cart. The mice curved their path and took the by-way toward Bayal.

Islam moved toward the mice with the whip in his hand. The mouse in the front was holding a big green candle in its mouth.

Islam who was laughing called Mashdi Baba. Mashdi Baba approached him. They bent down and looked.

"Look at those bastards; they're taking a candle to Bayal." Islam said.

"They take a candle there and eat two Kharwars[2] of wheat in return." Mashdi Baba said.

Islam started trampling the mice. The first mouse dropped the candle and ran away and the second mouse was crushed and squeezed under Islam's foot.

Mashdi Baba picked the candle up, looked at it, smelled it and said: "What shall I do with it?"

"Let's give it to the girl," Islam said, "she can keep it for her wedding night. How about it?"

"Very good," Mashdi Baba said.

They came back and gave the candle to the girl and lighted their pipes and sank in thoughts.

---

[2] A unit of weight. Approximately 900 pounds.

## 10

The Headman did his best, but Ramazan wasn't convinced to return to the village. He was sitting on the stone and saying: "Wait till mom comes and then we'll go."

"Mom is not coming for a long time." The Headman said, "She'll come after ten days."

"So we'll go after ten days." Ramazan said.

"What about our life, our works in the village?" the Headman said.

"You go if you want, I'll wait for her." Ramazan said.

The Headman sat down and wiped his sweat. The old woman's clothes were under his arm. Suddenly he stood up and said: "Listen, we can't sit here, let's go to the janitor of the hospital and wait for her there."

They rose and went to the janitor. The janitor had swept the threshold of the hospital and sprinkled water on it. He was sitting on a chair in front of the door and was eating lettuce.

"We took her to the hospital." The Headman said.

He winked to the janitor and continued: "They said she would come out after ten days. But Ramazan's not going to come back to the village."

"You go; I'll come with my mom." Ramazan said.

"All right Headman," the janitor said, "you go, Ramazan will stay here and help me, I'll send him back to you after a week."

The Headman picked up Ramazan's mom's clothes and gave Ramazan's returning car fare to the janitor and made him promise to send Ramazan back to Bayal right after a week.

Ramazan and the janitor went in. "You'll stay right here, in this room, till your mother comes back." The janitor said.

Ramazan put the bundle of yogurt and bread under the janitor's bed and sat on the windowsill. The janitor hid Ramazan's car fare under the lantern and went to bed and slept. Ramazan came out and sat on the chair and started eating lettuce.

## 11

When the Headman entered the village, Islam was washing the cart beside the pool. Papakh jumped down from the wall and ran barking toward the Headman to treat him, and sniffed him. Mashdi Baba's daughter went on the roof and saw that the Headman has come and is talking to Islam. She returned and picked up the dishes and passed the alleys hurriedly and went to the side of the pool and started washing and rinsing the dishes.

"Why didn't Ramazan come?" Islam said.

"He says I won't come till my mother comes." The Headman said.

Islam stopped and took a perplexed look at the fish and asked: "When will he come at last?"

"The janitor said that he'll send him back after a week." The Headman said.

Mashdi Baba's daughter counted: "How many days does a week mean?"

And tears filled her eyes.

"Wish you had brought him. You know that some people are waiting for him?"

And he signaled at Mashdi Baba's daughter.

Both of them turned and looked at Mashdi Baba's daughter. Mashdi Baba's daughter rose and picked up the dishes and started walking.

When she entered the alley, she saw that Papakh and Islam's black goat are looking at her with astonishment.

## 12

At nights the janitor slept, and each time a patient came and knocked on the door Ramazan would rise and open the door. The janitor had promised the Headman to send Ramazan back to Bayal right after a week, and on the sixth day he said to Ramazan: "I was at the hospital, they won't discharge your mother this soon. And also your father hasn't paid the fees for her treatment. Tomorrow you go to the village and bring money."

Ramazan accepted and it was agreed that he would go before the dawn. The night came earlier than usual. So the janitor and Ramazan went in the room earlier and closed the door to sleep. The wind was blowing. They heard Azar who had bent down from the window and was telling her children: "Do you see what the wind is doing?"

The wind picked up the filth and tainted cotton balls from the yard and took them out.

The janitor, without eating dinner, covered his head with the blanket and slept.

Ramazan sat down by the wall and watched the almond bough which was scratching the window pane.

The sounds were mixed and every once in minutes the doctor could be heard from the upper floor, who would open the door, cough in the corridor and curse. Ramazan fell asleep, aware of the sounds.

It was in the middle of the night when he woke up. A sound could be heard. A familiar sound could be heard. The sound of the bell could be heard from within the wind. He listened. The sound got close and closer and stopped in front of the outer door, and then a hand slowly fell on the knocker and softly knocked on the door. Ramazan looked. The janitor hadn't woken up. He opened the door of the room and went into the corridor. He heard the doctor coughing in his bed.

Ramazan went forward; somebody's panting could be heard from behind the door. When he opened the door he saw his mother who had new clothes on. Ramazan went out happily and took his mother's hand. The two of them walked away hurriedly. The wind was blowing wildly and pushing them forward. Other bells could be heard from afar.

"Where are we going mom? Are we going to Bayal?" Ramazan said.

"We're not going to Bayal." Mom said, "We're going to the violet-bed."13

In the morning, the Headman, Mashdi Baba and Islam got on the cart, went to the roadside and waited.

Papakh and Islam's black goat also went and stood beside the cart. The Bayalers came out from time to time, looked at the road from beside the pool and went back.

Around the evening, Mashdi Baba who was frowning asked: "Won't he come? Didn't you say that he'll come?"

The Headman anxiously answered: "he said that he would send him. But nothing's happened till now."

At night, Mashdi Baba's daughter came down from the roof, picked up the big green candle and came out of the house. She went toward the hill, to light it at the *Token*.

# Second Story

## 1

When the Headman climbed the wall, the men rose from the ground and stood. The Headman bent and looked at the men in the moonlight and jumped down and went to Islam and took his hand, they passed the darkness by the wall and went to Islam's house. The Headman stood by the window, Islam went in, folded the carpet and took it out from the window; they walked together and came to the side of the pool. They stopped under the willow and whispered in each other's ears for some minutes and then came to the men. First the Headman and then Islam climbed the wall and jumped to the other side. A few seconds later, they appeared again and both climbed the wall and looked at the people. The Headman said in a solemn voice: "*Fatiha*."[3]

Then the people understood; they prayed the *Fatiha* in a confused and astonished manner. Then, one by one, they climbed the wall and sat up there all around and saw that Islam's carpet is spread over the dead man and a little lantern is beside the corpse, and also a little bowl of water; and big, winged mosquitoes are flying around the lantern.

Islam and the Headman jumped down to the other side of the wall again, they called Mashdi Jabbar and Mashdi Safar's son.

"You must go to Seyedabad." The Headman said to Mashdi Jabbar.

"Now?" Mashdi Safar's son said.

"Yeah, right now." Islam said.

---

[3] A prayer for the guidance and mercy of God.

"Go to Seyedabad by Islam's cart," the Headman said, "to Haj Sheikh, and tell him that the Holy man has passed away and ask him to come for the prayer. Bring him. The Holy man himself has willed so."

Mashdi Jabbar and Mashdi Safar's son looked at each other and went toward Islam's house.

"Be careful not to let the goat out when you're getting the drawbars." Islam said.

"We're careful." Mashdi Safar's son said.

And they went away. Islam and the Headman came to the side of the pool and stopped by the pit in which was the black stone used for washing the dead. Mashdi Baba came and stood beside them and asked the Headman: "Do you think that Haj Sheikh can come?"

"Why not?", the Headman said, "If he finds out that the Holy Man is dead, surely he'll come."

"Because," Mashdi Baba said, "There's disease in Seyedabad and all of the people are gathered in the beggar lady's house, they take three or four corpses out every day."

"Who gave you the word?" the Headman said.

"Mir Ibrahim's wife, who had taken her daughter to the city with the Holy man's son, had noticed a tumult in Seyedabad while returning." Mashdi Baba said.

"Where's the Holy Man's son anyway?" Islam said, "Wouldn't he show up even now that his father is dead?"

"He's staying in his aunt's house." The Headman said.

"But the aunt is with the other women, isn't she?" Mashdi Baba said.

"Last night, when I went there I saw that he has made himself wholly at home in his aunt's." The Headman said.

"Why didn't you let him know before the holy man passed away?" Islam said.

"I would let him know." The Headman said, "You don't know how cheeky this Mir Ibrahim's wife is, she stared at my face and said: 'I won't let you take my nephew away and scare him to death.'"

"It's better that you didn't let him know." Mashdi Baba said.

"I didn't let anyone know." The Headman said, "I was alone when he passed away. At once I saw that his chest doesn't move any more. I took the lantern and I saw that it was finished. I came up and we fetched the rug."

"Now, what shall we do till morning?" Mashdi Baba said.

"We'll all stay awake." The Headman said.

"Yeah," Islam said, "it's impossible to sleep, it's almost morning."

The three of them walked by the edge of the pool, the women who saw the men were coming gathered and looked at them; Papakh who had waken up, was confusedly standing near the women.

"We'd better go and find Mr. Nassir." Mashdi Baba said.

"Yeah, let's go." Islam said.

The Headman in the front and Islam and Mashdi Baba after him went to the Holy Man's yard. The men were still sitting all around on the walls and looking into the yard. Islam climbed the wall and looked at the yard. It seemed to him that the dead body's chest was moving upward gently. He turned back and jumped down.

"What's up?" the Headman said.

"Nothing." Islam said.

The three of them passed the first alley and went toward Mir Ibrahim's house. The alley was quiet and empty. There was no noise, except their footsteps.

Islam opened the low door of the house. No one was in the yard. They returned and opened the little window of the room facing the alley. A big cat which was behind the window rose and shook itself and came out.

First the Headman and then Mashdi Baba put their heads in the room and listened. Someone was crying.

"Is he crying?" Islam said.

"How has he found out?" the Headman said.

Islam stroke a match, the room lighted up. Someone was standing at the end of the room and had put his head on the niche and was whimpering. First the Headman went in and then Islam. Mashdi Baba stood outside.

The Headman and Islam stood in the blackness.

"Mr., Mr. Nassir?" Mashdi Baba said from outside.

The man in the blackness coughed.

"Mr., we were looking for you," the Headman said, "Do you know that you must come back home?"

The black figure coughed again.

"Yeah," Islam said, "May I be sacrificed for your ancestor, you must come back home, now you are the holy man of the village."

The black figure cried loudly from within the darkness.

# 2

Mashdi Safar's son and Mashdi Jabbar, riding Islam's cart, were hurrying toward Seyedabad. Half of the path was downhill, they were moving fast. The wheels helped the horse to arrive sooner. From after *Shoor* only the horse pulled them, the men and the cart and the weight of the wheels.

When they were outside the village, Mashdi Jabbar said: "It's a pity the Holy Man died."

"I bet it is." Mashdi Safar's son said.

"Mr. Nassir is still a child. He can't take the holy man's place." Mashdi Jabbar said.

"Yeah, and a little child he is." Mashdi Safar's son said.

"He wasn't by the deathbed." Mashdi Jabbar said.

"No, he wasn't." Mashdi Safar's son said.

"They say he wouldn't come out of his aunt's house?" Mashdi Jabbar said.

"Yeah he has made himself too much at home in Mir Ibrahim's house." Mashdi Safar's son said.

"They say from the day they have taken his cousin to hospital he has been so absentminded." Mashdi Jabbar said.

"Yeah, my mom said so too." Mashdi Safar's son said.

"They say that pus flows out of the girl's knee, just like a tankard tube, and she can't walk anymore too." Mashdi Jabbar said.

"Why, she can walk. But they're right about the pus, it flows out, and a real flow it is." Mashdi Safar's son said.

"Wait a minute," Mashdi Jabbar said, "Maybe Mr. Nassir is in love with his cousin?"

"No idea," Mashdi Safar's son said, "perhaps he is, but the girl is sick and dying, you know that?"

"Yeah," Mashdi Jabbar said, "But it's still possible, isn't it?"

"It's possible." Mashdi Safar's son said.

"Curious times. Mr. Nassir is still a mere stripling." Mashdi Jabbar said.

"Not such a mere stripling." Mashdi Safar's son said, "He's more than fifteen years old."

"Some people are still a child even being fifteen." Mashdi Jabbar said.

Then both of them were quiet. They moved on and on until they arrived near a high and square stone which was fallen by the road like a pulpit. Mashdi Jabbar got off the cart and checked the wheels and made sure and said: "Let's go."

"Let's go." Mashdi Safar's son said.

Both of them got on, they turned the horses head and took the by-way to the *Big Mountain*.

"It'd be better to have an elder come with us as well." Mashdi Jabbar said.

"Yeah, and too better it would be." Mashdi Safar's son said.

"Haj Sheikh may be offended." Mashdi Jabbar said.

"Yeah, he may be offended." Mashdi Safar's son said.

"May God will that he's not out of Seyedabad." Mashdi Jabbar said.

"May God will." Mashdi Safar's son said.

"Has Haj Sheikh known that the holy man was sick?" Mashdi Jabbar said.

"No he hasn't." Mashdi Safar's son said.

"How shall we give the tidings?" Mashdi Jabbar said.

It was at the dawn when they got near Seyedabad. The houses were set upon each other half way on the mountain. There were hundreds of banners set on a house in the middle of the other houses. When the wind blew it made the banners flutter. Mashdi Jabbar and Mashdi Safar's son who were standing on the cart thought that the house was waving spontaneously. A Seyedabadian who had a big head appeared. Mashdi Jabbar called him. He came forward.

"Is Haj Sheikh in the village?" Mashdi Jabbar asked.

"Yeah, he is in the village. But he is sick, he is in bed." The Seyedabadian said.

"He's sick? What's wrong with him?" Mashdi Jabbar said.

"A lot of people are sick, it's more than a week that the disease has come. Till now, more than ten people have died." The Seyedabadian said.

"Why?" Mashdi Jabbar said.

"God knows why," the Seyedabadian said, "All the sick are gathered there for praying and getting cured."

He pointed at the banners.

"Is Haj Sheikh there too?" Mashdi Jabbar asked.

"He was in his own house till the last night, but he went there last night." The Seyedabadian said.

"Wasn't he well?" Mashdi Jabbar said.

"No, but something else had also happened to him." The Seyedabadian said.

"What had happened?" Mashdi Jabbar said.

"His son has run away with Mashdi Ommat-Ali's daughter and he's been sicker out of sorrow, he has gone there." The Seyedabadian said, "Don't tell anybody but he's gone there to hush the people."

The three of them turned and looked at the banners.

"Aren't you going to the village?" Mashdi Jabbar said to the Seyedabadian.

"Yeah, I am." The Seyedabadian said.

"Get on, then." Mashdi Jabbar said.

The Seyedabadian also got on the cart. The three of them moved and entered a wide alley in the middle of which was a large puddle full of mud. They had put stones around the puddle. They got off the cart and passed the stones and went to the other side.

"We've come from Bayal." Mashdi Jabbar said.

"I know," the Seyedabadian said, "and this is Islam's cart, isn't it?"

"Yeah, we've come to see Haj Sheikh." Mashdi Jabbar said. "We should go there now?"

He pointed at the banners. "Yeah," the Seyedabadian said, "you should go and see him in there."

"Where's there?" Mashdi Jabbar said.

The Seyedabadian gave him a surprised look and said: "Where? It's clear where it is. It's the Beggar lady's house."

Mashdi Jabbar and Mashdi Safar's son who had got the point, together said: "Aha! The Beggar lady's house!"

## 3

In the morning, the Headman and Islam climbed the wall. "Let's go to work Headman. Let's settle the affairs before Haj Sheikh is here." Islam said.

"Yeah, let's go." The Headman said.

The Headman and Mashdi Baba and two youths went to the Headman's house and got the shovel and the pickaxe and the ladder and went toward the graveyard.

Islam and Abbas and two other men went to Islam's house. They brought the broom and the waterskin and the enameled bowl and the bag and came to the side of the pool. Islam and Abbas put everything they had in their hands down by the willow and went to the pit in which was the black stone used for washing the dead. Islam and Abbas grabbed the corners of the stone and moved it. A little snake jumped out and threw itself into the pool. Two other men came and helped and they pulled the stone out of the pit and put it facing the Qibla and reinforced its position with pebbles.

"Good." Islam said.

"Yeah, it wouldn't move anymore." Abbas said.

"And it gets heavier day by day." Islam said to himself.

The women were gathered at the other side of the pool and were looking at the pool. A young boy who had no cap on his head and his red, kinky hair had come down on his ears, came out of the alley and gave Islam a large platter in which was a bundle, and said: "It's for the Holy Man."

"I know." Islam said.

And he took the platter and put it under the tree and put a stone on it, so as not to be blown away by the wind.

The Redhead walked away from the side of the pool and went to the back of Mashdi Safar's house. Mashdi Safar had put his head out of the roof-hole and he was watching the pool. His gaze passed the alleys and the willow-grove and reached the graveyard. He saw the Headman and Mashdi Baba and the youths who were digging a grave at the right side of the Stone Lion. It approached and sat on the Stone Lion and watched them.

Mashdi Baba who was shoveling the soil out said: "Shall I dig more?"

"You come out now. I'll dig the rest." The Headman said.

Mashdi Baba came out and the Headman went inside the pit. The Headman who was shorter than Mashdi Baba was disguised in the grave pit. Only the nozzle of his pick which was coming and going up and down could be seen. Mashdi Baba gave the shovel to the Headman. The Headman who was shoveling the soil out suddenly bent down and dug out a little enameled jar. He wiped the soil off it and held it up. Everybody walked forward. The jar had blue enamel and a little red fish was painted on the enamel. The Headman turned the jar upside down and shook it. A soft ash flowed out which made all of them cough. Except Mashdi Baba, who had drawn himself aside and was praying Fatiha.

## 4

Since the day Mir Ibrahim's daughter was brought to the hospital by her cousin and her mother, no empty bed had been found for her yet and she was laid in the garden under the old elm tree. A tall, old nurse who had bundled her hair under a blue kerchief would bring her soup at noon and rice with split peas to eat in the evenings. She had forgotten about all the pains and coughs. She just wanted to run away by any means and return to Bayal.

The night when the Holy Man died she was having a nightmare in which they had tied a rope to the holy man's corpse legs and a crowd was gathered and they wanted to recline it down into a big well. The crows had come and gathered on the roof of holy man's house and shook their wings and Islam's cart was stopped at the end of the alley, Mashdi Jabbar and Mashdi Safar's son were standing on the cart. Mashdi Safar's son was holding a bowl in his hands and a little red fish was circling around itself in the bowl.

When she saw all these, she woke up in horror and burst into tears. Her whimpering filled the whole garden. The old woman appeared. It was nearly dawn. She came running. A crowd rushed out of the halls and all of them coughed.

"Why do you cry?" the old woman said.

"It aches." Mir Ibrahim's daughter said.

"Where does it ache?" the old woman said.

The girl raised her hand and turned it in the air and first put it on her belly, then on her bosom and then hung her hand and put it on her knee which had been bandaged and the pus had leaked out of the dressing.

"Oh, I got it. My poor child." The old woman said.

It was getting light. The morning breeze which was blowing brought a delicate coolness. Single coughs could be heard from the halls now and then. The people had returned to their beds.

"Don't cry my child," the old woman said, "the doctors will be here right now, I'll go to them and see what I can do."

She sat there until the sun rose. The janitor opened the outer door and the crowd standing behind the bars rushed in. The janitor barred their way and half-closed the door. And the people returned and raised their hands and hung from the bars and while coughing, stared at the yard and at the narrow halls. The doctors came. The old woman took Mir Ibrahim's daughter by the hand and they climbed the stairs and went to a thin tall doctor who was standing in front of a mirror holding a handkerchief before his mouth and was coughing.

"What shall I do with her? Tell me, what shall I with to her?" the old woman said, "It's been more than a week that this child has fallen in our hands, under this sunshine. For God's sake!"

The doctor wiped the water off his eyes and said: "Go search in the halls. If you found an empty corner, embed her there. But I know that there's no room in the women's halls."

"What shall I do with her if no room was found?" the old woman said.

The doctor shrugged and while wearing his white blouse said: "How do I know, discharge somebody, if you have the power, and put this one in her place."

"I'll go and see." The old woman said.

"Look Granny Fatimah ," the doctor said, "they say some things about you. Is it true?"

"What do they say?" the old woman said.

"They say that everyday, when you go out, you take a big bag full of bread and food with yourself." The doctor said.

"Yeah, it's true." The old woman said.

"Why do you do that?" the doctor said.

"I collect and take with me the leftovers that they want to throw away." The old woman said.

"But how big is your stomach?" the doctor said.

"Me? ... God knows." The old woman said.

Then she and Mir Ibrahim's daughter came down the stairs and went to the first hall which was long and stuffy with benches clung to each other and lean bony women who were staring out with popped-up eyes. Both of them entered. A woman was coughing in her bowl. When the old woman and the girl approached, she rose and went out. The old woman stopped. She looked at the woman's empty place and pressed the girl's hand. Suddenly she let go of the girl's hand and went forward and saw that the bowl in the woman's hand is full of blood and she was going to empty it. They came out of the first hall. They went to the second hall which was messier and three patients were throwing another patient out. In the second hall, even under the beds were full. They came out.

"I'll take you to a nice place right now." The old woman said.

And she took her to the corner of the garden, under a large tree which had spread its boughs even outside the garden. There was a pit beside the tree and in the pit, a bundle of bread and leftovers.

"It's much better here." The old woman said.

The girl said nothing. "Wait, I'll make a nice bed for you." The old woman said.

She went away and returned with two gunnies which she spread under the tree and laid down the girl on them and said: "Now it's very nice."

The girl said nothing. "Whenever you felt hungry, you can eat these." The old woman said.

She pointed at the bundle.

The sun was shining on both of them from between the boughs and making them uneasy.

## 5

The Beggar lady's house was crowded. On the stairs and the Yard's floor, even on the ledges of the walls, the people were laying. The house sounded like a hive. They were all clung to each other, weeping and kissing the banners.

The Beggar lady, who was blind in both eyes, was sitting on a little stool in the middle of the upper chamber. She was turning her head slowly and listening to the weeping of the Seyedabadians.

Each time the weeping was cut in a corner, she would turn her head that way and the weeping would start again.

The men were gathered in the lower room. Haj Sheikh was sitting at the upper end of the room with a face and belly puffed many times more than the others. He had stretched his big swollen legs in the middle of the room; a big wooden rosary was hanging from his neck. His eyes were exploring the ceiling of the room.

A water-bearer in black and green clothes was walking among the people and giving water to thirsty ones.

Mashdi Jabbar and Mashdi Safar's son stood outside the room. The Seyedabadian went upstairs and cleared a path from between the people for himself and put his head in the room from upon the stairs and in a loud voice said: "Haj Sheikh Your Excellency!"

The weeping was cut and Haj Sheikh brought his head forward and stared at the window. "Haj Sheikh Your Excellency, two men have come to you." The Seyedabadian said again.

Haj Sheikh turned his head back and gave the Seyedabadian a sign with his hand to leave him at rest. "Two men have come to you. They've come from Bayal." The Seyedabadian said louder.

The Seyedabadian approached and Haj Sheikh, with a choked voice, asked: "What do they want?"

"I don't know," the Seyedabadian said, "they've come by Islam's cart. But I don't know them, they're young."

"Call them." Haj Sheikh said.

The Seyedabadian went out and came back with the Bayalers. Mashdi Safar's son and the Seyedabadian put their heads in. Mashdi Jabbar passed from among the people and stood between Haj Sheikh's swollen legs.

Haj Sheikh looked at him and said: "What's happened?"

"The Headman and Mashdi Baba sent their greetings and asked you to come to Bayal." Mashdi Jabbar said.

"Come to Bayal?" Haj Sheikh said.

He pointed at his swollen legs and belly.

"The holy man has passed away." Mashdi Jabbar said.

Haj Sheikh made a sudden move and half rose. The weeping was cut. Haj Sheikh stretched his arms so that Mashdi Jabbar could help him. The water-bearer also came. They raised Haj Sheikh up together, who slowly went to the window and to the yard by the window. They took his turban and his cloak. Mashdi Safar's son and the Seyedabadian and Mashdi Jabbar and the water-bearer all helped him to go out by the door of the yard. They passed the alley and arrived at the place where the cart was stopped. Islam's horse had dropped its head down and was dozing off. A big coffin was leant against the cart; Mashdi Safar's son and the water-bearer took the coffin and laid it down by the wall and they spread Haj Sheikh's cloak on the floor of the cart and made his turban into a pillow, they helped so that

Haj Sheikh got on the cart and laid down on the floor of the cart.

Mashdi Jabbar and Mashdi Safar's son sat in the front, on the driver's seat. Mashdi Jabbar turned back and looked at Haj Sheikh who was gazing at the sky; and his feet, as big as two waterskins, were hanging from the edge of the cart. The water-bearer and the Seyedabadian had gone to the other side of the puddle and were looking at them with narrowed eyes. The sun was higher in the sky, it was almost noon.

## 6

The Headman and Mashdi Baba returned to the village when they had finished their work at the graveyard. They saw Islam and Abbas who were sitting by the pool and smoking their pipes. The sun was spread over the trees; the fish had come to the surface of the water and were eating foam.

"No news?" the Headman said.

"No, he hasn't come yet." Islam said.

"We've done our job, it's finished." The Headman said.

"There's a lot of work to be done yet, I and Abbas have settled the things here." Islam said.

"Let's go and bring the corpse." The Headman said.

"No, first we better go and draw Mr. Nassir out by any means," Mashdi Baba said, "Bayal will be disgraced if Haj Sheikh comes and sees that the Holy Man's son is not over the corpse's head."

"Alright," the Headman said.

The youths went toward the yard and climbed the wall and sat beside the others.

The Headman and Mashdi Baba and Islam walked toward the aunt's house.

The window was open and the old woman had come and sat in front of it. The cat was also there which, seeing them, rose and shook itself and went away.

"Where is Mr. Nassir, auntie?" the Headman said.

"He's there; he's standing at that end." The aunt said.

The three men bent down and saw that Mr. Nassir is, as before, on foot and has put his head on the niche and is crying.

"Mr. Nassir, it's too late now, come out." The Headman said.

Mr. Mir Nassir didn't answer.

"Do you know that people want to offer their condolences to you? Come out." Mashdi Baba said.

"He must come out before the night by any means." Islam said to the Headman and Mashdi Baba.

"Don't tire yourself out," the aunt said to the Headman, "He won't come out. Leave him alone."

"I don't think he comes out." Mashdi Baba said.

The men turned back and started walking. "Why wouldn't he come out?" the Headman asked.

"He's grieving for the girl." Mashdi Baba said.

"Seek refuge in God," Islam said, "His father is dead and he doesn't care; but he's grieving for the girl!"

"How do we know that he knows that his father has died?" the Headman said.

They went back to the aunt. The cat had come and was lounging; it went away as soon as it saw them.

"Does the boy know that his father is dead auntie?" the Headman said.

"Maybe he knows." The aunt said.

"But what on earth is wrong with him? Why wouldn't he come out?" the Headman said.

"The night before last night he's had a nightmare that his cousin has died in the hospital." The aunt said.

"What can be done to take this nightmare out of his head?" the Headman said.

"We must go back to the city and find her and see if she's dead or not." The aunt said.

"When will you go back?" the Headman said.

"Today." The aunt said.

"Won't you wait till the Holy Man's funeral is over?" the Headman said.

"There's nothing we could do, do it yourselves." The aunt said.

"The cart is away to bring Haj Sheikh, how do you want to go?" Islam said.

"We didn't go by your cart the other time either," the aunt said, "We borrowed two donkeys from Mashdi Safar and went there. Because the girl couldn't walk; But this time we two go on foot."

"God bless you." The Headman said.

They turned back and went toward the yard. The sun had reached the middle of the sky. The Headman and Mashdi Baba climbed the wall and Islam who had nausea went and sat under the willow to refresh.

Mashdi Baba saw that the corpse had swollen. The Headman thought that the dead body had grown too big since last night.

"It's an offence," Mashdi Baba said to the youths, "It's been half a day that the body's left on our hands. It's better to take and wash it and, till the job is done, Haj Sheikh will surely show up."

"Yeah, let's go to work, it's an offence." The Headman said.

And he climbed the ladder down into the yard. He stood and thought, and loudly said: "How shall we lift him?"

Mashdi Baba looked from above and saw that the yard doesn't have a way out except a little hatch. "How had he come in?" he asked the Headman.

The Headman bent down and opened the hatch and said: "From here."

A narrow dark hall appeared. "How had he come in here?" Mashdi Baba said.

"He was alive then," the Headman said, "he had opened the hatch, bent down and come here, where it's been cool and cozy. But now, now, how shall we take him out?"

Mashdi Baba shook his head. "It's easy," Abbas said, "We take the coffin down and put the body on it and lift it right from here and take it to the pool."

"The coffin is big, it wouldn't get into the yard." The Headman said.

"We'll give it a try." Mashdi Baba said.

Abbas and the Redhead brought the coffin and took it into the yard from above. Mashdi Baba climbed down the ladder too. He and the Headman took the coffin and pulled it down. But the handles of the coffin were so long that they stuck into the wall and the coffin didn't come down.

"Didn't I tell you?" the Headman said.

"It's nothing; let's saw it a little." Abbas said.

"It wouldn't work, think of something else." The Headman said.

"The Headman is right," Mashdi Baba said, "The coffin wouldn't do, let's go bring some boards and put them under the body and put a rope under the boards and lift it."

"Mashdi Baba is right, that's very easy." The Headman said.

"O.k. then, we didn't know about that." Abbas said.

All of them sat down silently till the Redhead and Abbas came back with some boards and ropes.

The Headman and Mashdi Baba pulled the corners of the rug together. The men first spread the ropes under the body and put the boards on the ropes and gave the ends of them to those who were on the wall.

"Pull up gently, if you pull hard you'll all fall down from up there. You know that?" the Headman said.

They pulled the ropes. "Wait till we come up too." Mashdi Baba said.

They didn't pull the ropes. First the Headman and then Mashdi Baba climbed the ladder and stood on two corners of the wall. The others pulled the ropes. As the body was coming up, it became lighter. Its naked, swollen legs gathered the cobwebs from over the wall and left some grooves on the wall.

## 7

When they washed the body and wrapped it in a shroud it was long past noon. Tired, they were all sitting around the edge of the pool, looking at the water and the fish. The body was in the coffin and the coffin in the shade. They had folded Islam's rug and put it on the ladder. Nobody was talking. All of them were in thoughts when Papakh's barking rose and he came running to the head of the alley and scraped the earth. Everyone turned and looked. Then Islam's cart appeared with Mashdi Jabbar and Mashdi Safar's son on the driver's seat and Haj Sheikh sitting on the floor, big, he could be seen so big. The men stood up.

"Why does Haj Sheikh look like that?" Abbas asked.

"He's swollen, He's big." The Redhead said.

"Yeah, his head's swollen; his arms and belly are swollen too." Abbas said.

"Times bigger." The Redhead said.

"His turban, how ragged his turban is." Abbas said.

The cart came and stopped near the body. The Headman and Mashdi Baba went forward and wanted to say hello, they couldn't. They stood there, looking at Haj Sheikh who was half-risen and looking at the coffin with horror. Islam also went forward and stood. Suddenly Haj Sheikh took his turban off and hit it on the ground and roared. The men came forward and saw that Haj Sheikh's eyes were full of tears. It was the first time that someone was crying for the holy man's death. The men who had come to their senses started weeping and moaning. The women also started moaning from inside the houses and behind the walls. Wailing arose from all over Bayal.

Islam's black goat and Papakh ran away and went to the back of Mashdi Safar's house and they saw Mashdi Safar who had brought his head out of the roof-hole and raised his hands and was gazing at the pool, he was weeping bitterly and shedding tears all over his face.

## 8

It was almost evening when they returned to the village. Several youths had crutched under Haj Sheikh's arms and were helping him walk. Haj Sheikh had unwrapped his turban and hung it from his neck, his eyes were puffed and he breathed with difficulty.

When they came to the side of the pool, they saw that the women had set banners all around the square and were sitting under the willow in black chadors, and as soon as they saw the men their weeping and moaning rose. The men went to the holy man's house with dropped heads. They passed the first alley and reached the head of the second alley and then the holy man's house. The door was closed and a big sack of straw had been thrown on the threshold. Islam went forward and pushed the sack aside and put his hand into the hole beside the door and opened the door. He went in first and picked up the bricks which were heaped up in front of the hatch. The gloomy, dusty hall lighted up. They brought Haj Sheikh in and they moved toward the only room of the house which was large and dark, and only the faint light of the evening came in from the hole in the middle of the ceiling. Islam went to the niche, he lighted the lamp and brought and put it in the middle of the room. In the room there were two rugs and a Quran and a bowl and some onions and stale bread. And some pillows and quilts were heaped upon each other. The men stood in the hall, Haj Sheikh sat down on the ground and then slowly stretched his legs and then stretched his whole body, his chest was moving quickly and his lips were shaking. Everyone was standing and waiting.

"Call his son." Haj Sheikh said.

"He's gone to the city this noon." The Headman said.

"Poor Holy Man." Haj Sheikh said.

No one talked. "I'm being suffocated," Haj Sheikh said, "take me to the yard."

Mashdi Baba opened the hatch at the foot of the wall. A dark, narrow hall appeared. First he went in himself and then Haj Sheikh who had bent with trouble and after Haj sheikh the Headman. The others stood waiting in the room.

"Haj Sheikh is hungry," Islam said to Abbas, "fetch some broth from Mashdi Safar's house."

Abbas went out; the others also went out and stood in the alley. The Headman and Mashdi Baba took Haj Sheikh to the yard. The ladder was still leaned against the wall and the holy man's rug and pillow were still spread on the floor of the yard.

Haj Sheikh lied down on the rug. He was bigger than the Holy Man. The wick of the lantern was burnt to the end. The bowl of water was full of mosquitoes. Mashdi Baba took the bowl and poured the water on earth and went to bring fresh water.

"And bring the lantern here too, Baba." The Headman said.

"I'll bring it." Mashdi Baba said.

Then he picked up the lantern and bent down and went to the hall. The Headman looked at Haj Sheikh's swollen body and said: "God, how much he looks like the Holy Man!"

## 9

When it was dark, those who had come to the hospital's garden and were gathered in front of the halls went out in groups; the old woman had not shown up since early in the morning.

Mir Ibrahim's daughter was behind the bars, she was standing there and looking out and as soon as the janitor went to his room, she came out with the others. It was hotter out there. When she passed the turn in the street, an intense weakness overcame her and she sat on the stairs of a house and sank in thoughts.

An hour had passed from the night when the old woman appeared from the turn in the street; she was bent, carrying a heavy bundle on her shoulder. When she arrived in front of Mir Ibrahim's daughter she put the bundle down, took out a piece of bread and put a handful of rice on it and without showing any acquaintance, went to the other side of the street to give another beggar's share.

## 10

At night, all the people put on black clothes and came to the side of the pool. A blurred moonlight was cast on the willows and the low roofs of the houses. Everywhere was half-lighted.

Islam and Mashdi Jabbar rolled the black stone together and threw it into the pit. They waited until the Headman came and signed to Islam. Islam climbed the stone and cleared his throat and started chanting a dirge loudly. The men opened their shirt buttons and started crying. The women came on the roofs and shaking their heads in the radiance of moonlight, started weeping. First Papakh and then all of the dogs of Bayal went out and gathered in the small square at the back of Mashdi Safar's house and eavesdropped. Islam's black goat went to the closet and hid. That night Bayal chanted dirges and wailed until the morning.

## 11

The Aunt and Mr. Mir Nassir arrived in the city early in the morning and got off in a crowded square. Both of them were hungry and didn't have the strength to walk. Mr. Mir Nassir sat by a wall, under the shadow of an old umbrella rammed into the wall. His turban had been misplaced in the village, he had wrapped a green napkin around his head.

"Are you hungry?" the Aunt said.

Mr. Mir Nassir said nothing and coughed.

"We've got nothing to eat." The Aunt said.

Mr. Mir Nassir coughed again.

"We need to have something to eat to have power in our limbs," The aunt said, "You stay here and I go begging. Maybe we'll get something."

The aunt tied her chuddar around her waist and, bent double, started walking. She had put her hands on her back and her feet took off the ground with trouble.

Mr. Mir Nassir put his hands on his cheeks which were flushed by fever and while coughing, looked at the Aunt who was disappearing in the crowd.

## 12

The doctor who was walking in the garden of the hospital noticed Mr. Mir Nassir who, in ragged clothes and the green napkin around his head, was running here and there and looking everywhere.

He called the nurse and said: "See where this boy comes from."

The nurse went to Mr. Mir Nassir and said: "Where are you from?"

Mr. Mir Nassir said nothing and coughed.

"He doesn't speak." The nurse said to the doctor.

The doctor coughed and said: "Ask him from which ward he is?"

The nurse pointed at the halls and said: "From which of these are you?"

Mr. Mir Nassir coughed and said: "I want Zahra."

"Zahra? Who is Zahra?" the nurse said.

Mr. Mir Nassir coughed and said nothing. The nurse bent and looked in Mr. Mir Nassir's eyes and softly asked: "Who is Zahra?"

Mr. Mir Nassir shook his head and said nothing.

"Take and confine him to a bed." The doctor said.

The nurse took Mr. Mir Nassir to a dark hall full of people and sat him down on the corner of a rug and she came out and saw the old woman who was hurrying to the corner of the garden. She stopped her and said: "Granny Fatimah, one of the patients hasn't eaten and is hungry, do you have something to give him?"

"Of course I do!" the old woman said.

She took the nurse to the corner of the garden. She put a handful of rice on a piece of newspaper and cut a piece of bread as well and put it in the nurse's hand.

## 13

When the Headman climbed the wall, the men stood up. The sun had risen and Bayal was shining. The Headman looked at them and jumped down the wall and went to Islam. They passed from among the crowd and went to Islam's house. The Headman stood by the window. Islam went in. He folded the rug and took it out of the window. They came beside the wall together. First the Headman and then Islam climbed the wall and jumped into the small yard. Some moments later, they climbed the wall again. The Headman in a solemn voice said: "*Fatiha!*"

The men looked at each other and swallowed their tears and prayed Fatiha.

Islam called Mashdi Jabbar and Mashdi Safar's son and said: "Get on the cart and go to Seyedabad and let the Beggar lady know what's happened, then take the shortcut and go to Khatoonabad to Mr. Mir Hojjat and tell him that Mr. Haj Sheikh has passed away and, ask him to come for the prayers and bring him."

Mashdi Jabbar and Mashdi Safar's son looked at each other and started walking toward Islam's house.

"Take care that the goat doesn't get out like the other day." Islam said.

Mashdi Jabbar coughed and said nothing.

Islam and Abbas went to the pit to take out the black stone for washing the dead.

The Headman and Mashdi Baba went to Headman's house. They took the shovel and the pickaxe and went to the graveyard and started working on the left side of the Stone Lion.

And the Bayalers climbed the wall and sat all around and stared at the body which was fallen in the yard and little by little was swelling and becoming bigger.

# Third Story

## 1

About the evening, Granny Fatimah was sitting on the roof and watching a big blackness that was coming from Seyedabad. Granny Fatimah thought that maybe someone had died in Seyedabad and the Seyedabadians were going to *Jamishan* by Mashdi Roghayeh's cart to take Haji Akhoond to their village for the prayers. But the more the blackness got near the larger and wider it became. When it was by *Nabi Agha* hill, Granny Fatimah saw a dirty, black wind which was carrying something white with itself. She ran to Mashdi Safar's roof, put her head into the roof-hole and called Mashdi Safar's wife loudly: "Granny Khanoom! Granny Khanoom! Come on up here and see what on earth this is that's coming toward Bayal?"

She returned to their roof again, hung her legs into the hole and grabbed the edges of the hole with her hands and stared at the blackness with horror. On Mashdi Safar's roof, first appeared Granny Khanoom's head and then Mashdi Safar's, which came out slowly. Granny Khanoom was looking all around quickly and she couldn't see anything.
"There it is." Granny Fatimah said, "It's coming from Seyedabad, look at there. Look at *Nabi Agha*."
The wind was whirling around *Nabi Agha* and whirling the whiteness with it.

"How long has it been whirling there?" Granny Khanoom said.

"It appeared just right now." Granny Fatimah said.

Granny Khanoom narrowed her eyes and prayed and blew at Bayal and turned and said to Granny Fatimah: "Woe is us. We're miserable."

Both of them looked with horror at the blackness that was coming toward Bayal by the by-way.

"Do you see the whiteness?" Granny Fatimah said loudly.

"Yeah, I see them." Granny Khanoom said.

"It's growing bigger. It'll cover Bayal all over when it reaches here." Granny Fatimah said.

A sharp, dirty stink spread everywhere and then the wind entered the village and scattered a large amount of rags which it has brought with itself in the alleys and on the roofs.

"Go down Granny Fatimah, the stink is suffocating us." Granny Khanoom said.

"Come down to the edge of the pool." Granny Fatimah said, "Let's see what we can do."

Both of them went down. The village was empty and the men and the women had gone out.

Granny Fatimah and Granny Khanoom came to the front of Baba Ali's house which was a small enclosure with a hatch. And Baba Ali's loud moaning and weeping could be heard from within it.

"Do you smell the stink? What shall we do?" Granny Khanoom said.

"I'm afraid those who have gone out can't come back to the village." Granny Fatimah said.

"Do you see these?" Granny Khanoom said.

She bent and pointed at the rotten rags which the wind had brought and scattered everywhere. "It seems that it has passed from some graveyards and has collected all and brought them here." Granny Fatimah said.

And while shaking with horror, she sat on the black stone for washing the dead and leaned against the willow.

Granny Khanoom also sat down and pulled her legs under her chuddar, not to let the cold wind wrap the rags around her thin shanks.

"The knell is rung for everything." Granny Fatimah said, "First the famine and then this."

Baba Ali's moaning rose louder from within the enclosure. Granny Khanoom pointed her hand and said: "Do you see?"

"Let's get up and go let everybody know." Granny Fatimah said.

"But there's nobody left in the village." Granny Khanoom said, "Besides, Mashdi Islam must come and let everybody know!"

"I'm worried, I'm very worried, Hassani's away and hasn't returned." Granny Fatimah said.

"My son is away too, no need to worry." Granny Khanoom said, "Everyone will return, let's go home, light lanterns and take them on the roofs so that the lost ones can see Bayal."

They rose to go. A man appeared from the blackness by the Landlord's garden. He had a large basket in his hand and had humped his back and was approaching by the rim of the wall on tiptoes.

Granny Fatimah took Granny Khanoom's hand and said: "Who's this Granny?"

"As for me, I don't know him." Granny Khanoom said.

The black figure came and passed by and went to the first alley.

"He was walking so noiselessly, what if he goes to my house?" Granny Fatimah said.

"Let's follow him." Granny Khanoom said.

The two old women followed the black figure into the alley on tiptoes. They passed the turn in the alley and saw that the black figure has stopped in front of Mashdi Jabbar's house and is coughing. The door opened and Mashdi Reyhan, Mashdi Jabbar's sister, appeared with a lantern. The black figure drew aside, Mashdi Reyhan raised the lantern. The light of the lantern was cast into the alley and it lighted the rotten rags which were sticking to the doors and the walls and were shaking. Granny Fatimah and Granny Khanoom drew themselves aside and stood in the darkness.

"Who's that?" Granny Fatimah asked.

"Mashdi Reyhan, Mashdi Jabbar's sister. The one whose husband is dead." Granny Khanoom said.

They took several steps forward and stopped. The black figure put his hand into the basket hanging from his arm. He took out a beheaded chicken which he was holding by the legs and held it before the lantern. Mashdi Jabbar's sister stretched her arm and took the chicken by the legs and went in and closed the door. The black figure took his path again and went to the end of the alley. And Granny Khanoom and Granny Fatimah followed him. When the black figure reached Granny Fatimah's house, he stopped, stretched his arm and took a short rope which was nailed into the wall, and pulled himself up.

"Where's he going?" Granny Fatimah said.

"Wait a minute!" Granny Khanoom said.

The black figure reached the roof. He bent and threw his basket in from the roof-hole and then put his legs into the hole and hauled himself down slowly. Only his head remained out which looked at the pool for some moments and suddenly fell inside the house.

"What shall we do now?" Granny Fatimah said.

"Come, let's fetch lanterns." Granny Khanoom said.

Both of them turned and took each other's hand and ran to the side of the pool. Pieces of rags were shaking on the willow boughs. Some people who were coming with baskets in their hands appeared from within the blackness. Granny Fatimah and Granny Khanoom went to Granny Khanoom's house. Mashdi Safar was standing on the stool, his body was completely in the room and just his head which couldn't be seen was out of the roof-hole. Granny Khanoom and Granny Fatimah went to the closet and picked up two lanterns and came to the room. They lighted both of them. Granny Khanoom went on another stool and put one of the lanterns on the roof. Mashdi Safar's body which was motionless moved and his fingers waggled. Granny Fatimah and Granny Khanoom came out with the other lantern. There was a crowd by the side of the pool. The Bayalers were entering the village with half-empty baskets. Islam was sitting on the cart and had sunk in thoughts.

Granny Khanoom went beside the cart and said: "Mashdi Islam, somebody has come and he's in Granny Fatimah's house."

"Isn't Hassani in the village?" Islam said.

"No, he's not; he's gone out." Granny Fatimah said.

"O.k. then, I'll come with you." Islam said.

When they reached Granny Fatimah's house, Islam took the lantern and opened the door. He went in first and the old women followed him. It was dark in the room. When they opened the window, Islam put the lantern in; someone was leaning against the wall and looking at them from within the darkness.

"Who are you?" Islam said.

"It's me Mashdi Islam." The black figure said.

Islam raised the lantern and said: "You?"

The black figure came forward, he had a basket on his arm, the three of them moved forward, "Is it you Hassani?" Granny Fatimah said.

Hassani put his hand in the basket and brought out a beheaded chicken which he was holding by the legs. The chicken's head was hanging from a narrow strip of skin and was shaking.

"Don't you know your own son Granny Fatimah?" Islam said.

He gave the lantern to Granny Khanoom and hurried out. Granny Fatimah stretched her arm and took the chicken from Hassani's hand.

"I couldn't get more than one." Hassani said.

He laughed boisterously, in a way that the old women were terrified and backed off.

## 2

Most of the men had returned empty-handed. Mashdi Jabbar had got some potatoes from "Khatoonabad"; before he would show up, Mashdi Reyhan had hidden the beheaded chicken behind the firewood.

"Khatoonabad was so crowded." Mashdi Jabbar said.

"But nothing's going on in Bayal." Mashdi Reyhan said.

"It's because something can be found there." Mashdi Jabbar said.

"Mashdi Baba who had gone to Khelijan has come back empty-handed." Mashdi Reyhan said.

"Many people have come back empty-handed," Mashdi Jabbar said, "Abbas had got a little rice from Seyedabad, half of which he took for himself and his sister and gave the rest to Baba Ali."

"Mashdi Hassan has only got an armful of grass which he took to the stable and gave to his cow." Mashdi Reyhan said.

"And hasn't the Headman returned yet?" Mashdi Jabbar said.

"Now, what are you going to do?" Mashdi Reyhan said.

"Tonight I'm going to go to Pooruss, maybe I can get something." Mashdi Jabbar said.

"You're going to go to Pooruss all alone?" Mashdi Reyhan said.

"Yeah, who else can I go with?" Mashdi Jabbar said.

"But you can't go alone." Mashdi Reyhan said, "After the midnight, Poorussians gather up and watch for their village."

"I'll go and avenge myself by any means." Mashdi Jabbar said. "I'll take vengeance for the sheep they stole from me."

"Not alone, you shouldn't go alone." Mashdi Reyhan said.

"I can't go with anybody." Mashdi Jabbar said, "The Bayalers all go begging, they cry, they collect alms, but they don't steal. Likewise, if the Poorussians starve to death they don't go begging and they don't collect alms, and they don't stop stealing either."

"I know, but what if they caught you?" Mashdi Reyhan said.

"But, nobody would come with me." Mashdi Jabbar said.

"Why, maybe Granny Fatimah's son comes." Mashdi Reyhan said.

"You're talking about Hassani?" Mashdi Jabbar said.

"Yeah, if you tell him, he'll surely come with you." Mashdi Reyhan said.

"How do you know?" Mashdi Jabbar said.

"I know," Mashdi Reyhan said, "When he came to the village an hour ago, he had a chicken in his hand."

"You mean he had been to Pooruss?" Mashdi Jabbar said.

"I think so, you sit here and eat your dinner, and I'll go and call him." Mashdi Reyhan said.

Mashdi Jabbar sat down and in front of the firewood and put the lantern beside him. Mashdi Reyhan brought him bread and wheat porridge and then went out of the house. The wind was still blowing. The men were gathered beside the pool and were saying prayers. From behind the short wall, a raw of women had raised their heads and were looking at the men. Someone was crying in Landlord's garden.

When Mashdi Reyhan reached Hassani's house, she saw Granny Fatimah and Granny Khanoom who were coming out with a bowl of holy water. Mashdi Reyhan drew herself aside. Granny Fatimah and Granny Khanoom came to the alley. Granny Fatimah was dipping a little broom she had in her hand into the holy water and sprinkling it on the doors and walls of the houses and she was praying. Granny Khanoom was crying loudly. As soon as the old women passed the turn in the alley, Mashdi Reyhan stepped out of the darkness and opened the door and went in. Hassani was sitting in front of the lantern by the window, eating porridge.

Mashdi Reyhan went forward and said: "Hassani! Hassani!"

"Why did you come here?" Hassani said.

"Get up and come with me." Mashdi Reyhan said.

"Where shall I come?" Hassani said.

"Mashdi Jabbar has come, he's going to go to Pooruss to steal chickens, and I told him that you would go with him." Mashdi Reyhan said.

"How shall we go at this time of the night?" Hassani said.

"Mashdi Jabbar's going to go," Mashdi Reyhan said, "you'll come back sooner if you go with him, and then you can sleep in our house."

"Will Mashdi Jabbar let me sleep in your house?" Hassani said.

"Yeah, but he won't let you if it is in the daytime." Mashdi Reyhan said.

"Alright, I'll come." Hassani said.

Both of them came out. Hassani put the last morsel of his dinner which was in his hand in his mouth and said: "You go, I come after you."

"We can get out of the village and take the path behind the Landlord's garden and go to the little square at the back of Mashdi Safar's house and then go to the first alley and then to our house if you like." Mashdi Reyhan said.

"Let's go." Hassani said.

It got colder when they were at the end of the alley and outside the village. The flickering of several candles could be seen at *Nabi Agha*.

"You can come to me whenever you're hungry; I keep something for you and myself." Mashdi Reyhan said.

"I'll come whenever I'm hungry." Hassani said.

"It's so cozy and quiet outside the village." Mashdi Reyhan said.

"Yeah." Hassani said.

"Let's sit on this stone." Mashdi Reyhan said.

They sat on a boulder fallen on the edge of a narrow valley.

"When you came back from Pooruss, you'll come to our house." Mashdi Reyhan said.

And Hassani said: "Yeah, I'll come."

"Mashdi Jabbar sleeps like a log." Mashdi Reyhan said, "He doesn't wake up, no matter what you do to him."

From within the darkness, a huge man came out who was dragging a thin, long sheep after himself. The moon appeared from the rents of the clouds. Mashdi Reyhan and Hassani recognized the Headman.

# 3

When Granny Khanoom and Granny Fatimah reached the side of the pool, the men had finished their prayers.

Islam had climbed the black stone for washing the dead and was chanting a dirge. Two lanterns were burning by the willow.

Islam was silent when he saw the old women. The men also became silent.

Granny Fatimah dipped the broom into the holy water and, she shook it first over Islam's head and then over the heads of all men one by one. "Do you see what misery has befallen us?" Granny Khanoom said, "On the one hand famine and hunger and on the other this new misfortune."

Mashdi Baba coughed, and Islam loudly said: "Forgive us Lord of the two worlds."

The men dropped their heads down and cried.

"Now, what are you going to do?" Granny Khanoom said.

The women who had stretched their necks from behind the wall craned more.

"Those who have got healthy bodies must raise arms and consider the others too." Mashdi Baba said.

"Mashdi Baba is right," Abbas said, "But anyone who finds anything takes it to his own house or puts it in his own mouth."

"Abbas wants to tell you that he has given a handful of rice to Baba Ali today, know you! All people!", Mashdi Safar's son said.

"All these apart, what shall we do tomorrow?" Mashdi Hassan said.

"We must gather several men and send them to Khatoonabad to get potatoes and wheat." Islam said.

"Seyedabadians and Hassanabadians have rushed to Khatoonabad and have collected and taken with them everything they could put their hands on." Mashdi Safar's son said.

"We'll go too, maybe we can find something." Islam said.

"We must have our cattle and sheep in mind too." Mashdi Hassan said.

"First let us fill the people's stomach." Mashdi Jabbar said.

"O.k., how do you want to go to Khatoonabad?" Abbas said.

"By the cart, when shall my cart come in handy if not now?" Islam said.

"Which ones want to go?" Mashdi Jabbar said.

"I'll hit the road early in the morning. Anyone who likes comes with me." Islam said.

"I'll come with you." Mashdi Safar's son said.

"I'll come too." Abdullah who had just arrived said.

"We can't go if we're more than three." Islam said.

"Yeah, three men are enough," Mashdi Baba said, "we'll collect money tomorrow and will give you sacks and bags and in the morning you shall go under God's protection."

"Mashdi Islam, I'll give you money so that you buy a bag of straws for my cow too, if you could find any." Mashdi Hassan said.

"I won't let Islam get straws for you if I go." Mashdi Safar's son said.

Islam signed to Mashdi Hassan and Mashdi Hassan said nothing. "When will we set out?" Abdullah said.

"Before the dawn." Islam said.

"Send someone to wake me up if I was late." Mashdi Safar's son said.

"All right." Islam said.

When the talk was over they all stood there, quiet and waiting. Granny Khanoom went forward and said: "It's settled. Three young men are going to fetch potatoes and provisions. What are the rest going to do? Are you going to go begging again?"

"It can't be helped Granny Khanoom," Mashdi Baba said, "We have to feed the children by any means."

"No." Granny Khanoom said, "No one is going out of the village tomorrow. Tomorrow we'll mourn. We'll beg for mercy, we'll cry, we'll wail. Maybe His Holiness pities and forgives us and takes the misfortune away from Bayal."

Granny Fatimah pointed at the willow from whose boughs pieces of rags were hanging and she said in a solemn voice: "Don't you see?"

And she started crying and dipped the broom in the holy water and shook it over the men's heads.

"Forgive us Lord of the two worlds." Islam said aloud.

The men dropped their heads down and the women who were lined upon the wall, hid behind the wall again and the noise of their crying rose.

"Their Excellencies won't forgive us unless a mourning ceremony is held." Granny Khanoom said.

"I and Granny Khanoom will go and sprinkle holy water on the entire village and then we'll bring the banners out from the banner-house." Granny Fatimah said.

The old women passed by the men and went toward the first alley. Papakh's moaning rose from within the Landlord's garden. The old women took the turn into the alley, and they saw Baba Ali's big hand which had come out of the hatch of the enclosure and was searching for something in the dust.

"O God, have mercy on us." Granny Khanoom said.

"Forgive us Lord of the two worlds." Granny Fatimah said.

At the end of the alley, the Headman appeared who was dragging a thin, long sheep after him.

## 4

Mashdi Reyhan and Hassani were sitting on the boulder by the valley when the old women appeared with the bowl of holy water and the broom. Granny Khanoom was praying and Granny Fatimah was sprinkling holy water all around the village.

"Here they are, let's go." Mashdi Reyhan said.

"Who?" Hassani said.

"The old women are here; let's go." Mashdi Reyhan said.

Both of them stood up. Mashdi Reyhan took Hassani's hand and pulled him into the valley.

"Where are you going? It's so dark down there." Hassani said.

"Come on, let them pass and then we'll go back home." Mashdi Reyhan said.

Hassani and Mashdi Reyhan were going into the darkness of the valley when the moon appeared from the rents of the clouds. The old women saw two black figures which were going into the valley.

"Did you see them?" Granny Khanoom said.

"Yeah, I saw them." Granny Fatimah said.

"Who were they?" Granny Khanoom said.

"God knows." Granny Fatimah said.

"Let's go, we have holy water with us, nothing happens." Granny Khanoom said.

"As for me, I'm not going into the valley." Granny Fatimah said.

"I'm not going either," Granny Khanoom said, "We'll look from above there and sprinkle holy water into the valley."

The old women came to the side of the stone on tiptoes and lurked and then both of them bent down into the valley. Hassani and Mashdi Reyhan were sitting by each other at the bottom of the valley. Mashdi Reyhan had put her hand on Hassani's knee. Both of them were looking upward when two heads appeared from the edge of the valley.

"What if they come down?" Hassani said.

"They can't." Mashdi Reyhan said.

"And if they came?" Hassani said.

"We'll run away from this side." Mashdi Reyhan said.

"Get up and let's go." Hassani said.

"Wait till they pass." Mashdi Reyhan said.

"Who are you?" Granny Khanoom shouted from above the valley.

Hassani and Mashdi Reyhan didn't answer.

"They don't answer." Granny Fatimah said.

"Are you human? Are you jinn? Speak, whatever you are." Granny Khanoom shouted.

Again, Hassani and Mashdi Reyhan didn't answer.

Granny Fatimah dipped the broom into the holy water and shook it into the valley.

"That's my mother." Hassani said.

"And that other one is Mashdi Safar's wife." Mashdi Reyhan said.

They were silent. Granny Fatimah was walking on the edge of the valley and sprinkling holy water.

Granny Khanoom bent over the valley and shouted aloud: "Whoever you are, human, jinn, whoever; I swear you to go away from here; go away from Bayal."

Hassani and Mashdi Reyhan didn't answer. The old women went back. "Let's walk quickly; we have a lot of work to do." Granny Fatimah said.

And Granny Khanoom said to herself: "It's so good that Mashdi Jafar is going to Khatoonabad with Islam. And that Mashdi Safar is asleep now. Really, what if Mashdi Reyhan made love to my son as well?"

When they were taking the turn to the alley, they turned and looked back. Two black figures came out of the darkness of the valley and sat on the boulder again.

# 5

When Mashdi Reyhan and Hassani entered the house, Mashdi Jabbar had wrapped himself in a quilt and had fallen asleep in front of the firewood. Mashdi Reyhan went forward and shook Mashdi Jabbar.

"What?" Mashdi Jabbar said while still asleep.

"Get up; Granny Fatimah's son is here." Mashdi Reyhan said.

"So what?" Mashdi Jabbar said.

"Don't you want to go to Pooruss?" Mashdi Reyhan said.

Mashdi Jabbar woke up and said: "Where is he?"

"I'm here Mashdi Jabbar." Hassani, who was standing by the door, said.

"I'm going to Pooruss, will you come with me?" Mashdi Jabbar said.

"Go to Pooruss to do what?" Hassani said.

"What one goes to Pooruss to do? We're going stealing." Mashdi Jabbar said.

"You say we're supposed to go stealing?" Hassani said.

"Yeah," Mashdi Jabbar said, "Do you remember that the Poorussians stole three sheep from me?"

"I remember." Hassani said.

"We're going to avenge it together." Mashdi Jabbar said.

"We need ropes. You know that?" Hassani said.

Mashdi Jabbar rose, he brought two ropes and gave one to Hassani and took one himself.

"Let's go." Hassani said.

"Tie the rope around your waist." Mashdi Jabbar said.

"I take it just this way." Hassani said.

"We'll be back before the dawn." Mashdi Jabbar said to Mashdi Reyhan.

"Come back sooner." Mashdi Reyhan said.

Hassani and Mashdi Jabbar came out. They passed the alley and reached the pool. The men were gone. Only some people had gathered around the pool and were chatting. The moon was shining into the pool from the rents of the clouds. The fish had come up and were eating foam.

When Hassani and Mashdi Jabbar reached Landlord's garden, Mashdi Safar's son appeared with several bags.

Mashdi Jabbar and Hassani passed by him silently.

"God speed! Where are you going at this time of night?" Mashdi Safar's son said.

"We got work to do." Mashdi Jabbar said.

Mashdi Safar's son laughed and said: "I know what kind of work you've got."

"Ok, good for you." Mashdi Jabbar said.

"I want to tell on you; that you're going stealing." Mashdi Safar's son said.

"What about you? Don't you want to come?" Mashdi Jabbar said.

"Never!" Mashdi Safar's son said.

"Better for you to shut up now." Mashdi Jabbar said.

Mashdi Safar's son was afraid, and he laughed.

"Go proclaim it; go tell everyone that Jabbar and Hassani went stealing." Mashdi Jabbar said.

When Mashdi Safar's son went away he cried: "Don't worry, I won't tell anyone."

Hassani and Mashdi Jabbar came out of the village. Mashdi Jabbar untied the rope from around his waist too, and hung it on his back. Hassani hung the rope on his back too. They took the by-way.

"If Mashdi Safar's son talks like that just one more time, I'll crush his teeth." Mashdi Jabbar said.

"Don't mind him. He's always talking nonsense." Hassani said.

"But we're not going stealing; we're going to avenge my sheep." Mashdi Jabbar said.

"And if we couldn't find any sheep, we'll steal chickens." Hassani said.

"Of course we do that." Mashdi Jabbar said.

When they climbed down the first hill, they saw three Poorussians who were pulling a battened sheep stolen from Seyedabad, taking it toward their village.

"God grant you strength." Mashdi Jabbar said.

"Beat it." One of the Poorussians said.

# 6

Granny Khanoom and Granny Fatimah pushed the stone door of the banner-house. Granny Khanoom put the lantern in; she looked at the low, dark hall. After her Granny Fatimah entered who was pressing the bowl of holy water and the broom against her bosom. They moved forward slowly. The lantern was casting light on the walls of the hall. All of the large and small niches on the walls were filled with fragments of Quran. When they reached the end of the hall, a small low door appeared which was covered with nailed-down pieces of lucky charms. Granny Khanoom started praying and Granny Fatimah dipped the broom in the water and sprinkled it on the door. Granny Khanoom opened the latch of the door. A dark crypt appeared. The old women both stood there for some seconds and looked at the darkness. First Granny Khanoom entered and after her Granny Fatimah. The crypt was filled with the smell of dampness and rottenness.

"How many banners are we taking out?" Granny Fatimah said.

"We're setting banners all around the pool." Granny Khanoom said.

"Can we take them out just by the two of us?" Granny Fatimah said.

"Of course we can." Granny Khanoom said.

Granny Fatimah put the bowl and the broom on the ground. Granny Khanoom took the lantern forward. Banners were put all around the room. Granny Fatimah put her hands on her bosom and Granny Khanoom was praying and blowing while passing in front of the line of the banners.

"But we can't touch these;" Granny Fatimah said, "All of them are rotten and will shake down if touched."

"I have no business with these." Granny Khanoom said.

They passed between two heaps of banners and reached a small zarih[4] fallen by the wall. Both of them sat beside the empty zarih. Granny Khanoom tore off a corner of her scarf and while tying it to the zarih, said: "O Fatimah Zahra, I beg for your mercy, I tie it here so that you take the misfortune away from Bayal."

"O Fatimah Zahra, I beg for your mercy." Granny Fatimah said.

She tore off a corner of her chuddar and tied it to the zarih; both of them stood up.

"Are we taking the banners?" Granny Fatimah said.

"We take them right now." Granny Khanoom said.

"Which ones are we taking?" Granny Fatimah said.

"Those that are behind the Icon." Granny Khanoom said.

Then she put the lantern on the ground. The two of them went toward the large icon which was leant against the banner.

---

[4] A lattice structure that encloses a grave. Similar to a mausoleum.

Granny Khanoom kissed the curtain of the icon and said: "Your Holiness, I beg for your mercy."

And Granny Fatimah said: "O Your Holiness, I beg for your mercy, save Bayal."

When they drew the curtain aside, His Holiness appeared who was standing up with two swords in his hands. Granny Fatimah and Granny Khanoom picked the icon up and put it before the zarih. The lantern lighted up the new banners.

The old women went toward the banners.

"I beg for your mercy, O Imam of the time." Granny Fatimah said.

"Forgive us Lord of the two worlds." Granny Khanoom said.

## 7

Mashdi Reyhan was sitting in the middle of the kitchen and she had put the chicken in hot water and was plucking it; a burning lantern was on the firewood. Papakh had come and was sitting at the other side of the open hatch and was staring at Mashdi Reyhan's hands with hung lips. Mashdi Reyhan was happy and she enjoyed the noises outside. When she tore the chicken's stomach up, Papakh's neck stretched into the kitchen.

Mashdi Reyhan put her hand into the stomach and disemboweled the chicken and looked. She rose and threw it out over Papakh's head and Papakh jumped down. Mashdi Reyhan cut the chicken into pieces and put it all in the copper pot and hung it in the kiln. She ate a bowl of porridge and then made a bed for Mashdi Jabbar in front of the firewood and behind it, for Hassani. Then she came and stood under the roof-hole and looked at the sky in which the moon had come out from the rents of the clouds. Then she took her own quilt and went to sleep behind the door so that she could wake up whenever

Hassani and Mashdi Jabbar came. She also brought the lantern and put it behind the door; she sat before the lantern with kohl-pot and mirror and put kohl on her eyes.

# 8

Hassani and Mashdi Jabbar arrived in Pooruss.
"What will they do to us if we get caught?" Hassani said.
"We won't get caught." Mashdi Jabbar said.
"Aren't we going into the village then?" Hassani said.
"No," Mashdi Jabbar said, "We're not going into the village. We'll sit in a corner around here and wait and when the Poorussians are coming back from stealing, we'll block their way and grapple it out of their hands."
"Can we?" Hassani said.
"Of course we can." Mashdi Jabbar said.
Both of them went and sat under one of the trees. The houses of Pooruss were quiet and no moving creature could be heard.
"Everybody's asleep." Hassani said.
"These people pretend to be sleeping." Mashdi Jabbar said.
"Do you see anything?" Hassani said.
"Look at that corner." Mashdi Jabbar said.
Both of them looked, the light of a pipe could be seen from within the darkness in the trees.
"Are they on watch?" Hassani said.
"Let them be," Mashdi Jabbar said, "Don't talk, sit down and let's see what happens."
"Ok, I won't talk anymore." Hassani said.
Both of them sat down silently; a cold wind was blowing. The sound of a bell could be heard from afar.
Mashdi Jabbar and Hassani looked. A small cart was moving toward Seyedabad from Khatoonabad.

"Do you see the cart?" Hassani said.
"Yeah," Mashdi Jabbar said.
"Why doesn't it have a driver?" Hassani said.
"It's Ok," Mashdi Jabbar said, "one sees lots of these things at night. But suppose that you haven't seen it at all."
"I'm afraid." Hassani said.
"Don't talk." Mashdi Jabbar said.
The cart went away and the sound of the bell was cut. The light of the pipe could no more be seen from within the darkness.
"Mashdi Jabbar!" Hassani said.
"What's wrong with you this time?" Mashdi Jabbar said.
"Maybe they haven't gone stealing tonight." Hassani said.
"How do I know?" Mashdi Jabbar said.
"Let's go back to Bayal." Hassani said.
"Why did we come then?" Mashdi Jabbar said.
"So get up and let's go into the village." Hassani said.
They came out from under the tree. They tied the ropes around their waists and took the by-way to the village.
The houses were compressed next to each other and quiet. When they passed before the windows, they could hear the breathing of the people who were sleeping calmly.
"What to do now?" Mashdi Jabbar said.
"Look for wells." Hassani said.
"Wells?" Mashdi Jabbar said.
"Yeah, the Poorussians hide the stolen stuff in wells." Hassani said.
"Let's look for wells, then." Mashdi Jabbar said.
"How many wells do you want?" Hassani said.
"The more the better." Mashdi Jabbar said.
"Ok, take my hand and we'll go into the darkness." Hassani said.

Mashdi Jabbar, who couldn't see clearly, took Hassani's hand. Hassani pulled him forward.

When Hassani stopped Mashdi Jabbar also stopped.

"What happened?" Mashdi Jabbar said.

"There we are." Hassani said.

"As for me, I can't see anything." Mashdi Jabbar said.

"Sit down." Hassani said.

Mashdi Jabbar sat down in the darkness and Hassani also sat down. Both of them were silent for a few seconds.

"Stretch your arm." Hassani said.

Mashdi Jabbar stretched his arm. A large, deep pit was under his hand from which a cold wind was blowing upward.

"Is this the well?" Mashdi Jabbar said.

"Yeah," Hassani said.

"Yeah, I can see. And a large well it is." Mashdi Jabbar said.

"There are even very larger ones." Hassani said.

"I'm sure you've been here many times." Mashdi Jabbar said.

Hassani laughed and didn't answer. Both of them bent down and looked into the well.

"What's this? What smell is this?" Hassani said.

"It's the smell of sheep, the smell of my sheep, the smell of my own sheep." Mashdi Jabbar said.

"Yeah, it smells of sheep, of sheep and something else too." Hassani said.

"Ok, what to do now?" Mashdi Jabbar said.

"One of us must go into the well." Hassani said.

"All right," Mashdi Jabbar said, "You hold the rope firmly and I go down."

"I'm afraid of darkness," Hassani said, "You hold the rope and I go down."

"But, isn't it dark in the well?" Mashdi Jabbar said.

"But you can't find any Poorussians down there." Hassani said.

"All right." Mashdi Jabbar said.

He untied the rope from around his waist and tied it around Hassani's waist. Hassani, sitting, hung his legs into the well and put his fingers on the wall of the well and crept into the darkness. Mashdi Jabbar let go of the rope little by little, and little by little Hassani sank into the darkness. Mashdi Jabbar looked around him. Everywhere was light and only he was sitting in the thick darkness and had the end of the rope in his hand. The rope was gradually becoming heavy and heavier.

"Hassani is tying the rope around the sheep." Mashdi Jabbar said to himself.

He bent down and smelled again. The smell of the sheep and the smell of Bayal were coming up from the well.

He bent over the well and softly said: "Hassani! Hassani!"

Hassani gave the rope a jerk from within the darkness. Mashdi Jabbar pulled the rope up. When Hassani came up, he had two beheaded chickens with him.

"Where are the sheep?" Mashdi Jabbar said.

"There was no sheep in the well." Hassani said.

"Just these two chickens?" Mashdi Jabbar said.

"Yeah, just these two." Hassani said.

"What if they're rotten?" Mashdi Jabbar said.

Hassani smelled the slashed throats of the chickens and said: "Today's."

"Let's go to another well." Mashdi Jabbar said.

Hassani looked at the moon which had come out from the rents of the clouds and said: "Now we must go back to Bayal."

"Why?" Mashdi Jabbar said.

"It's almost midnight," Hassani said, "It will get light till we reach there."

"When will we take the sheep?" Mashdi Jabbar said.

"Another night, anytime we came." Hassani said.

They tied the ropes around their waists. They put the beheaded chickens in the basket. Hassani took the basket; and as they were going away from over the well, the groan of a sheep was heard from the bottom of the well.

## 9

Granny Fatimah and Granny Khanoom were rescuing the banners from the darkness. The old women of Bayal had put black clothes on and were gathered in front of the stone door of the banner-house. Mashdi Zeinal was sitting on a heap of dust with his crutches and he was reciting Quran loudly. Granny Khanoom had left the lantern in the banner-house and she and Granny Fatimah were carrying the banners on their shoulders together, passing the dark corridor and coming to the front of the door. They first brought out the palm of the banner and then the banner itself. The old women of Bayal rushed and took the banners. Mashdi Zeinal would loudly say: "Praise and greetings on God's beloved."

The women would praise and pray and pick the banners up. Mashdi Safar, who had brought his head out of the roof-hole, was watching the pool and anytime the moon appeared from the rents of the clouds he would fix his eyes on the banners.

Mashdi Safar was watching the forest of banners.

## 10

Islam and Abdullah and Mashdi Safar's son were dallying with the cart beside the pool.

"Nothing's wrong with the cart, we can go as far as Khatoonabad." Islam said.

"Are you sure we won't get stuck in the middle of the way?" Abdullah said.

"I have traveled through Khatoonabad and Hazavan and Jamishan and Hassanabad by this four wheels and nothing has happened." Islam said.

"May God will that nothing happens this time as well." Abdullah said.

"The horse must be fine, the cart moves anyway." Islam said.

"The Headman always says so too." Abdullah said.

Islam looked at the bags and said: "What are all these bags for?"

"Each house has given one Toman[5] and two bags." Mashdi Safar's son said.

"Is that much potato likely to be found in Khatoonabad?" Islam said.

"They've taken us for free porters." Mashdi Safar's son said.

"Looks like that you're not so happy, you don't have to come if you don't want to." Islam said.

Mashdi Safar's son laughed and stretched himself over the sacks and said: "I come if I like and I won't if I don't."

Islam went under the cart. He checked the ropes and came out and said to Abdullah: "We'll hit the road if the Headman comes."

Mashdi Safar's son, who was looking at the moon and the rents of the clouds, said: "Mashdi Islam, do you know that Mashdi Jabbar and Granny Fatimah's son have gone to Pooruss for stealing?"

"None of my business, none of your business, none of our business." Islam said.

"I saw them myself." Mashdi Safar's son said.

---

[5] Toman is a unit of money.

"You shouldn't have." Islam, who was dallying with the shafts, said.

Mashdi Safar's son said nothing. Neither did Islam and Abdullah. Mashdi Hassan's cow could be heard from far away, and also a stranger dog which was coming toward Bayal, howling.

## 11

It was past midnight when Mashdi Jabbar and Hassani entered Bayal. Banners had been set all around the pool and nobody was out. Two kids were sitting under a banner and were eating wheat porridge.

When Hassani and Mashdi Jabbar took the turn into the alley, they heard the snoring of those who were sleeping. On one of the roofs, Granny Fatimah and Granny Khanoom were standing, each holding a very large banner in her hands.

"I'm fainting with fatigue." Mashdi Jabbar said.

"In a little while the sun will rise." Hassani said.

Mashdi Jabbar yawned again and said: "We walked four parasangs[6] and returned with two chickens."

"We can eat broth and wheat porridge." Hassani said.

They reached Mashdi Jabbar's house. They pushed the door. Mashdi Reyhan who was sleeping behind the door heard it; she woke up and drew herself aside. First Mashdi Jabbar and after him Hassani with the basket entered. The smell of chicken broth had filled the kitchen.

"I'm fainting with fatigue." Mashdi Jabbar said.

"Come, go to bed and sleep." Mashdi Reyhan said.

Mashdi Jabbar walked forward; he saw his quilt and pillow spread in front of the firewood. He took his cap off and lied down. The kitchen was warm. The broth was boiling in the kiln

---

[6] Parasang is a unit of itinerant distance, similar to the European "league."

noisily. He blinked. Papakh, with its wooly face, was sitting at the other side of the hatch and was looking at the kitchen.

"Hassani, take care you don't take the plump chicken for yourself." Mashdi Jabbar said.

"I don't want any; I give you both of them." Hassani said.

"Give them to Mashdi Reyhan, come and eat the broth tomorrow, if you liked to." Mashdi Jabbar said.

Hassani handed the basket to Mashdi Reyhan and Mashdi Reyhan put the basket on the firewood.

"I'm going home." Hassani said.

"I've made you a bed, at the other side of the firewood." Mashdi Reyhan said.

"Mashdi Jabbar will be angry if he knows." Hassani said.

"He sleeps like a log; he won't wake up till the blaze of the noon." Mashdi Reyhan said.

Mashdi Jabbar's snoring arose and following it, voices of a group of people from beside the pool who were mourning and crying.

"Shall I sleep here?" Hassani said.

"I've cooked broth for you; I'll bring it for you to eat." Mashdi Reyhan said.

Both of them went to the other side of the firewood which was a little enclosed space with a hatch, opening into the alley. The sky and the high roofs of Bayal could be seen from there. Hassani sat down on the quilt and looked at the moon which had come out from the rents of the clouds and he said: "It doesn't move, no matter how much I look at it, it doesn't move."

The sound of pot and spoon was heard. The whole kitchen was filled with the smell of broth. "I'm hungry, I'm so hungry." Hassani said to himself.

Footsteps and crying were heard from outside. Hassani looked at the alley. They were carrying a banner from behind the hatch. Large copper palms which were pointing at the sky with parted fingers. He heard his mother who was saying loudly: "I swear your Holiness, O, Ali, O, Muhammad, save Bayal."

Mashdi Reyhan came with the full pot and sat down beside him. Hassani looked at the pot. What was in the pot couldn't be seen.

"Is it too hot?" Hassani said.

"No," Mashdi Reyhan said.

And she took Hassani's hand and dipped his finger into the broth which was tepid.

He picked the pot up and said: "Don't you eat?"

"You eat and I'll eat too." Mashdi Reyhan said.

Hassani quaffed the pot. The broth was salty and oily. It smelled of wheat and of well.

"Did you like it?" Mashdi Reyhan said.

Hassani nodded and gave the pot to Mashdi Reyhan. Mashdi Reyhan took the pot and took one or two gulps and passed it over to Hassani again. Hassani finished the broth and put the pot on the ground.

"Do you want some porridge?" Mashdi Reyhan said.

"Not any more, I won't have anything." Hassani said.

Mashdi Reyhan rose and picked the pot up and said: "Now lay down."

She put her hand on Hassani's bosom and laid him down. The quilt was soft and the firewood smelled of toasted bread. Hassani stretched himself. Mashdi Reyhan picked the pot up and went to the other side of the firewood. Hassani rolled and suddenly his eyes caught hundreds of tiny eyes which were looking at him from within the firewood. He told himself: "As for me, I'm really full. If you were not mice, Mashdi Reyhan would give you broth too."

And he laughed and rolled again and faced the hatch. A banner was standing back there and its large palm was pointing at the sky with two long fingers.

"O your Holiness, O Muhammad, O Ali." Hassani said.

The palm moved away. Hassani turned over and took a breath and closed his eyes. Mashdi Reyhan approached on tiptoe and went under Hassani's quilt. Mashdi Jabbar was weeping bitterly in his sleep.

## 12

From Seyedabad, Hassanabad, Malekzadeh, Yengijeh, Jamishan and Mishoo, the row of carts had set out toward Khatoonabad. From every corner of the desert, sounds were taking the tired horses of the carts and the hungry men, all panting, toward Khatoonabad.

Khatoonabad was awake. Mashdi Enayat the headman was searching and peeping into every house. The Khatoonabadians were hurriedly pouring potatoes into bags and throwing the bags into the wells.

The sound of the wheels turning fast, the sound of the panting of the hungry people moving toward Khatoonabad, and the sound of the bells which were threateningly whirling around the village…

## 13

Mashdi Jabbar was having a nightmare in which he was descending into a large well in Pooruss. A rope was tied around his waist. But no one was over the well to hold the rope. The rope had come out from the rents of the clouds. He was hanging from the moon.

When he reached the bottom of the well, he smelled Bayal. He smelled his sheep which Poorussians had taken away from Bayal three years earlier. When his eyes were accustomed to the darkness, he moved forward. But three Poorussians with unsheathed daggers blocked his way. Behind their backs the row of the sheep and the chickens were waiting.

"Where are you going?" the first Poorussian said.

The second Poorussian waved his dagger and said: "Where?"

The third Poorussian said: "We'll cut off your head, your head."

"I want my sheep." Mashdi Jabbar said in a solemn voice.

The three Poorussians surrounded him and said: "We want the chickens, the chickens."

"My sheep, my sheep." Mashdi Jabbar said.

The Poorussians attacked him and raised their daggers and said: "We'll cut off your head, your head."

"Pull me up! Pull me up!" Mashdi Jabbar shouted with horror.

He woke; a cold sweat had covered his body. The group of mourners was passing from the alley in the back.

Mashdi Jabbar heard Islam who was crying and singing loudly:

"The thirsty-lipped Hussein's head,

See it on the earth of Karbala."

And the Bayalers would softly and mutely repeat:

"The thirsty-lipped Hussein's body,

See it on the earth of Karbala."

Mashdi Jabbar half rose and looked at the empty hatch. Then he came to the side the firewood. He looked at the hatch facing the alley. Copper palms with spread fingers were passing one after another. Mashdi Jabbar came forward; a big copper palm with two long fingers came and stopped in front of the hatch.

Granny Khanoom's voice was heard from the alley who was weeping: "I beg for your mercy, take the misfortune away from Bayal, O, Imam, I beg for your mercy, O, Prophet, I beg for your mercy."

The sound was cut when the palm moved away. As Mashdi Jabbar was turning back, he saw that Hassani had fallen asleep and Mashdi Reyhan was laid beside him, she has put her hands around Hassani's neck, like copper palms.

Mashdi Jabbar hurriedly went to the other side of the firewood and brought the lantern and bent down. When the light was cast on Hassani and Mashdi Reyhan's faces, suddenly both of them opened their eyes.

Mashdi Jabbar crushed the lantern on the ground and roared: "Oh, oh, oh!"

He ran out and latched the door from the other side. Hassani and Mashdi Reyhan stood up.

"Do you see what happened?" Hassani said.

"Come on, let's run away, let's run away." Mashdi Reyhan said.

Hassani and Mashdi Reyhan went toward the door. The door was locked from outside. Mashdi Jabbar's voice could be heard from outside who was running around the house and yelling: "Oh, oh, oh!"

"Do you hear?" Hassani said.

"He's running?" Mashdi Reyhan said.

"Where to?" Hassani said.

Mashdi Reyhan opened her arms and said: "Just like this, around the house."

"What shall we do? What shall we do?" Hassani said.

They came to the back of the firewood again and looked at the alley. The big copper palm with two long fingers had come and was standing behind the hatch; someone was coughing in the alley.

Mashdi Jabbar was running around the house and yelling: "Oh, oh, oh!"

From beside the pool the mourners could be heard who were groaning:

"The thirsty-lipped Hussein's head,
See it on the earth of Karbala.
The thirsty-lipped Hussein's body,
See it on the earth of Karbala."

"Come on, come faster." Mashdi Reyhan said.

Hassani moved; Mashdi Reyhan lifted a boulder next to the kiln. A dark stairway appeared.

First she and then Hassani went into the darkness. And when they came into the alley, Mashdi Jabbar was standing beside them and yelling: "Oh, oh, oh!"

Hassani and Mashdi Reyhan froze in their places. At the other side of Mashdi Jabbar Abbas appeared who had the palm of a banner in his hand. Mashdi Jabbar turned and when he saw himself between the three, he took several steps backwards and yelled with horror: "My sheep! My sheep!"

The mourners sang from beside the pool: "The thirsty-lipped martyr's head, the thirsty-lipped martyr's body."

And Abbas cried and said: "Hussein's head, Hussein's body."

## 14

When they reached "Shoor", Mashdi Safar's son jumped down from the cart and said: "I'm not coming any further."

He tied a thick rope which he had with him around his waist and hung his basket from his arm and took the by-way to Pooruss.

Islam and Abdullah looked at him for a while and then hooted the cart toward Khatoonabad. The desert was drilled and in every hole a mouse's head could be seen which were looking out with tiny, waiting eyes. When they saw the shadow of the cart, they would go down and come up again.

When Islam and Abdullah arrived in Khatoonabad, they were dumbstruck by the large number of the carts. Inside and outside the village, the carts were stopped from one end to the other and men with heaps of bags were sitting on the carts. Mashdi Enayat was passing among the carts and saying aloud: "By God, nothing's left, we have nothing."

When he saw Islam he came to him and said: "Do you want potatoes too Mashdi Islam?"

"Yeah Mashdi Enayat, there's a sorry plight in Bayal." Islam said.

Mashdi Enayat pointed at the carts and said: "Do you see?"

"What shall I do?" Islam said.

"Go and wait in a corner," Mashdi Enayat said, "Maybe I could find something for you."

Islam turned the horse's head back; they came to the roadside and stopped there. Abdullah opened his kerchief and took out wheat porridge for them to eat together. From inside a pit near the cart, the big hand of a Khatoonabadian beggar came out and spread open before Abdullah and Islam.

Islam put a handful of porridge in the beggar's hand. When the hand went into the pit, several mice came out.

## 15

Mashdi Reyhan and Hassani were roaming in the city. The scent of toasted bread was spread everywhere. Both of them were full, with an armful of bread; they were watching the houses. When the sun curved, they went to a ruined house and sat down beside a pit.

"How hot it is in the city!" Hassani said.

Mashdi Reyhan, who was rubbing her hand against Hassani's thigh, said: "And what a tasty bread we got."

## 16

Islam's cart was stopped at the by-way. With the palms and banners which set all around the cart. Islam, the Headman, Mashdi Baba, Abdullah and Mashdi Hassan were searching in the valley in darkness. Seyedabad was asleep. The Bayalers had come for donkey's carcass. There were several carcasses in every valley. But they wanted fresh carcass which they found and put it into a big basket and all the five men dragged it out of the valley.

When they got on the cart, they had surrounded the carcass. The donkey's wrinkled eyes were open and it was looking at the moon which was shining from the rents of the clouds. The mice had rushed out and filled the desert. When the wheels of the cart ran over them they screamed. Mashdi Baba could hear the cracking of their bones.

Bayal appeared from a distance, with the candles and a fire which had been lighted at *Nabi Agha*.

"May God impart it not even upon blasphemers." The Headman said.

"But as far as I know, He has imparted it upon us." Islam said.

"If we had found an armful of grass, my cow…" Mashdi Hassan said.

"Thank God at least we're not returning empty-handed." Abdullah said.

"O God, thank for what you have granted, thank for what you have not granted." Mashdi Baba said.

When they arrived in the village, the Bayalers came out, beating their breasts, carrying large banners. All of them were mourning and crying. Granny Fatimah and Granny Khanoom were in front of all, who with bent statures, chains around their necks, each were carrying two large banners on their shoulders.

Granny Fatimah was lamenting:

"The martyr of Karbala's head,

The martyr of Karbala's body."

And the hungry crowd yelled:

"The thirsty-lipped martyr's head,

The thirsty-lipped martyr's body."

When Islam saw the crowd, he covered his face with his hands and started weeping bitterly. The crowd circled around the cart and stared at the donkey's big, damp carcass with appetite and became quiet.

It was just past midnight. A stranger's voice was saying Azan from far away.

And the dogs of Bayal were howling ceaselessly.

# Fourth Story

## 1

When Mashdi Hassan's wife came out, the sun had newly risen. Islam had brought his cart to the side of the pool and was waiting for the Headman to come so they could go to Khatoonabad to Mashdi Enayat's sister' funeral. The Headman had gone to Mashdi Baba's house; he wanted to take him with them too. But Mashdi Baba was excusing himself. It was because Mashdi Enayat didn't like him, he wanted to get rid of the Headman at any cost when, suddenly, they heard Mashdi Hassan's wife crying from near the pool.

"Who's crying?" the Headman asked.

"Yeah, someone's crying!" Mashdi Baba said.

He climbed the ladder hastily and put his head out of the hole over the door and looked. He saw Mashdi Hassan's wife who had tied her black chuddar around the neck and was stretched on earth beside the pool, beating her fists on her head ceaselessly and crying. And Islam was standing several steps from her and perplexedly looking at her.

"What's up?" the Headman asked.

"Mashdi Hassan's wife has come to the side of the pool," Mashdi Baba said, "She is beating herself and crying."

"Why?" the Headman asked.

"How do I know, maybe something has happened to Mashdi Hassan." Mashdi Baba said.

"But Mashdi Hassan is not in the village, he's gone to Seyedabad to labor." The Headman said.

"So, has the woman gone mad, tearing herself apart like that?" Mashdi Baba said.

The Headman raised his head and listened. Mashdi Hassan's wife was weeping and yelling so hard that the headman couldn't stand it anymore and he ran out and Mashdi Baba stood on the ladder just as he was and again put his head out of the hole over the door. When the Headman reached the pool, the Bayalers rushed out and came there in surprise; they stared at Mashdi Hassan's wife and looked at each other.

Islam had bent and was repeatedly asking Mashdi Hassan's wife: "What's up? What's happened?"

And Mashdi Hassan's wife cried: "Oh, oh, oh, I'm miserable!"

First Granny Khanoom and the Headman and then all Bayalers went and gathered around Mashdi Hassan's wife. In the pool a chicken's carcass was swimming, around which the fish were turning and swallowing the tiny bits of fat floating on the water.

Granny Khanoom, as soon as she reached there, sat down face to face with Mashdi Hassan's wife and asked: "Mashdi Touba, Mashdi Touba, what's happened sister? Tell me what's happened?"

Mashdi Hassan's wife stretched out on the earth when she saw the crowd. Her face pulled together and her nose twinged with pain and two strings of tears were flowing down from her eyes.

The Headman bent down and asked: "Granny Khanoom, has something happened? Eh? Has something happened to Mashdi Hassan?"

"She can't talk, she's fainted," Granny Khanoom said, "Back off all men, back off, set a piece of cloth on fire and give it to me."

Abbas' sister set a piece of cloth on fire and gave it to Granny Khanoom. She took the cloth and twisted it. The flame fainted inside the cloth and a black smoke rose. The men went and gathered under the willow. And the women came and circled around Mashdi Hassan's wife.

"Take her hands, shake her." Granny Fatimah said.

Two women sat down and took Mashdi Hassan's wife's hands and shook them and Granny Khanoom held the cloth before her nose. After some moments Mashdi Touba opened her eyes, she sat up and looked around her and suddenly burst into tears and groaned loudly: "Oh, oh. Ah, oh. I'm miserable."

The men came closer, and the Headman came and stood beside Granny Khanoom and asked: "Ask her if anything's happened to Mashdi Hassan?"

"Give her some water to drink," Granny Khanoom said, "she can't talk unless she drinks water."

The Headman came nearer and asked Mashdi Hassan's wife: "Let me see sister, is Mashdi Hassan well?"

One of the women brought water in a bowl. Granny Khanoom took the bowl and said: "Drink, drink some water so that you can talk."

Mashdi Hassan's wife half-rose and said: "I can tell without drinking water. I can tell. I can tell that I'm miserable."

"Surely some misfortune has happened to Mashdi Hassan." Islam said to the men.

The men nodded. Granny Khanoom gave the bowl of water to Abbas' sister and said with surprise: "She can tell without drinking water? How can she tell without drinking water?"

## 2

The men in the back and the women in the front came closer and circled around Mashdi Hassan's wife and stood waiting.

"Mashdi Islam, Mashdi Islam, has something happened?" Mashdi Baba shouted from the hole over the door.

Islam signaled him with his hand to be silent. Everyone bent down. Mashdi Hassan's wife wiped her eyes with the corner of her chuddar and said: "The cow, the cow!"

"The cow?" Islam asked, "What's wrong with the cow?"

"Last night, last night, Mashdi Hassan's cow has died last night." Mashdi Hassan's wife said.

The men turned with surprise and looked at each other. Granny Khanoom stood up suddenly and said: "What? What did you say?"

"When I went to water her in the morning, I saw that she'd stretched out on the earth and her limbs were stretched too, and her mouth was full of blood." Mashdi Hassan's wife said.

The men turned and looked at Mashdi Hassan's house.

The women whispered and Granny Fatimah said: "O Imam of the time."

"But why? Was anything wrong with her?" Granny Khanoom said.

"No, nothing was wrong with her," Mashdi Hassan's wife said, "when I went to the stable at night she was standing at the pen, fit as a fiddle, and was grazing."

"How do we know that there hasn't been an evil eye on her?" Baba Ali said from among the men.

"They have put an evil eye on her? Who would do that?" Islam said.

"You don't understand. May God save everyone from evil eyes." Baba Ali said.

Granny Khanoom sighed and said: "Amen, Lord of the two worlds."

The Headman coughed and took his cap off and rubbed his hand on his head and said: "How do we know that a snake hasn't bitten it?"

"Islam! Mashdi Islam! Has something happened?" Mashdi Baba shouted from the hole over the door.

Islam signaled him with his hand to be silent. Mashdi Touba opened her arms and imploringly said: "What shall I do now? What on earth shall I do now?"

Mashdi Safar's son loudly said: "Whatever you do and whatever kind of dust you put on your head, if it's dead it won't come alive again till the Day of Judgment."

The Headman turned and looked at Mashdi Safar's son. Again Mashdi Hassan's wife said: "But what shall I do? If Mashdi Hassan comes back and sees that his cow is dead he'll have a heart attack at once."

Islam turned and looked at the empty road and Mashdi Baba who had newly arrived asked Islam: "Has something happened? Mashdi Islam, has something happened?"

The Headman put his cap on his head and turned toward Islam and said: "She's right, if Mashdi Hassan comes back and finds out that his cow is dead, you know in what mood he will be."

"How can we help it?" Islam said.

"I don't know; you know better than all of us." The Headman said.

Islam climbed the black stone for washing the dead and said: "The headman said that when Mashdi Hassan returns, no one should tell him that his cow is dead."

"No one will tell him," Mashdi Safar's son said, "But when he returns and he can't find his cow he'll know that it's dead. Am I right Mashdi Islam? Am I right Mashdi Baba?"

Islam who was standing on the black stone for washing the dead was perplexed, and said: "He's right Headman, if he comes and he can't find the cow, what can be done about that?"

"What can be done about that?" the Headman said.

Islam said to the crowd in a loud voice: "The Headman says that no one should tell Mashdi Hassan that his cow is dead, his spouse will tell him that his cow…"

Mashdi Safar's son interrupted Islam and said: "Will tell him that his cow is dead."

"Mashdi Jafar, would you let Mashdi Islam talk?" the Headman said.

"His spouse will tell him that the cow has run away and Ismail's gone to find it." Islam said.

The men were silent. Islam climbed down the stone and said: "What shall we do now Headman?"

"I don't know what we shall do!" the Headman said.

Islam turned and said to the men who were staring at him, surprised: "The Headman says that some men must come to go to Mashdi Hassan's house to see what can be done with the cow."

When Mashdi Baba heard that, he went to the edge of the pool, he started taking out the chicken's carcass out of the water with a stick he had in his hand.

# 3

Islam and the Headman and Abbas and Ismail and Mashdi Jabbar and the Redhead went to Mashdi Hassan's house and Mashdi Hassan's wife, crying and beating on her head, followed them. The sunshine was cast on the pole in the middle of the stable from the roof-hole; it had cast light on a smoky lantern and a dirty rope.

Mashdi Hassan's cow was dropped in the middle of the stable and had stretched out her limbs in a way as if a tired man was sleeping. Her large eyes, half-open, were staring at the holes on the corner of the wall. Her nozzle was full of blood and it seemed that a twisted rope had been crumpled into her throat.

The Headman bent down and looked at the cow's eyes. Islam and Ismail went and sat beside the carcass. Ismail rummaged in the blood-stained ropes in the cow's mouth with a stick he had in his hand. A sound was heard from the cow's throat. It looked like that the beast's throat opened up and some of the ropes went down gurgling.

Mashdi Hassan's wife said: "Dou you see how miserable we are Headman? Do you see Ismail? Do you see Mashdi Islam? Do you see my misery? Do you see?"

"There's no God but Allah," the Headman said, "What can be done?"

"Yeah," Islam said, "The die is cast, now we must be aware that Mashdi Hassan doesn't hurt himself."

Ismail coughed and said: "It's all over for Mashdi Hassan now; he can't get on his feet and be a man anymore."

"May God have mercy." Mashdi Jabbar said.

Mashdi Hassan's wife sat down and leaned against the pole and started crying.

Islam turned and looked at Mashdi Hassan's wife and said to Ismail: "Tell her not to cry, tell your sister not to do something that Mashdi Hassan notices it."

Ismail went and sat down before Mashdi Touba. He took out his pipe and lighted it and said: "Sister, Mashdi Islam tells you not to cry, the Headman tells you not to cry too, don't do something that gives a hint to Mashdi Hassan. Take this and have a puff so that you come to your senses."

Mashdi Hassan's wife swallowed her sobs and took the pipe from Ismail. Ismail returned to the men. The Headman walked around the cow's carcass and said: "Wish more men had come with us."

"Where do you want to take her?" Islam said.
"We'll skin it and then take it out." Mashdi Jabbar said.
"When will Mashdi Hassan be back?" Islam said.
"He'll come today. Sure he'll come back today." Mashdi Hassan's wife said, while sobbing.

Islam sat down by the wall and took his cap off and rubbed his hand against his head and said: "We won't skin her, he may arrive suddenly and then things will be worse."

"You're right, we shouldn't do that." Ismail said.
"Where shall we take it to?" Mashdi Jabbar said.
"Yeah, where shall we take it to?" the Headman said.
"We'll take and throw it into the valley." Abbas said.
"No, the valley won't do, he may go there and find her." Islam said.

The Headman coughed and said: "Yeah, Mashdi Hassan passes through the valley and goes to the desert every day."

"No, we won't take it to the valley." Islam and Ismail said together.

The Headman coughed again and said: "Isn't it better to take it to Shoor Mashdi Islam?"

"Shoor? You mean we take her there?" Islam said.
"Yeah, isn't it better?" the Headman said.
Islam thought and said: "No, you know Headman, the news will echo in the entire neighborhood and at last he'll hear about it."

"What shall we do now?" the Headman said.
Islam rose and took the bricks out of the hole in the stable wall; the sunshine came in and cast light on the pen and the cow's carcass. Mashdi Hassan's wife made a move and tied her chuddar around her waist tightly and coughed.

"Where's your well Mashdi Khanoom?" Islam said.
Mashdi Hassan's wife turned and said: "In that corner."

And she pointed at the front of the pen.

"All right," Islam said, "Let's throw her into the well."

He stood up and took his cap off and put it on the pen. The men also rose. Islam said to the Redhead: "Run and bring the shovel and pickaxe from the Headman's house."

The Redhead went out like the wind. All the men rose, put their hats on the pen and came and circled around the carcass. Something was whistling inside the cow's throat. When they looked, they saw the blood-stained ropes which had come up again and had filled the cow's nozzle.

## 4

When they took the dust away and put the stones aside, a large well appeared. Islam threw a stone into the well. The men all listened. Then they rose and went to the carcass.

"Can we lift it?" Ismail said.

"He's right," Mashdi Jabbar said, "Are we strong enough to lift it?"

"We won't lift her," Islam said, "We'll just drag and take her to the edge of the well."

They took the carcass's hind legs and tail and dragged it to the edge of the well. Islam and Ismail and the Redhead stood on one side of the well and the Headman and Mashdi Jabbar and Abbas on the other side of the well. They put the carcass's hind legs and tail on the edge of the well.

"You two take care; I and Ismail push it down." Islam said.

The Headman and Abbas sat on the edge of the well and put their feet on the carcass's rump and waited.

Islam and Ismail and the Redhead went to the upper end, they pushed the carcass forward a little.

"Take care not to fall in." Ismail said.

The Headman and Abbas were afraid and drew back a little. The carcass moved forward again. The Headman and Abbas put their feet on the rump and pushed it into the well. When the carcass was in the well up to the waist, the Headman and Abbas also rose and came to Islam and Ismail and the Redhead and the five of them got busy. The more they moved forward, the easier the carcass would hang in the well, and when they reached the edge of the well, they let go of the fore legs. The cow, its fore legs still raised, fell into the well with open eyes. The five of them bent down and looked. A noise was heard from within the darkness and at last the sound of something flowing, as if the nozzle of a waterskin had been opened, that flowed and flowed and was finished.

# 5

When Mashdi Hassan came home, Abbas and his sister were sitting and were talking with his wife. Mashdi Hassan put his bundle on earth and took is shoes off and threw them before the window, he greeted Abbas and said to his wife: "Have you given water to the cow?"

Mashdi Touba didn't answer.

Mashdi Hassan said: "Should this poor animal give up the ghost out of thirst if I'm not in this ruined house for a single day?"

And he picked up the empty bucket from upon the platform and ran out toward the pool. Islam had washed his cart and was fastening the shafts when he saw Mashdi Hassan and greeted him loudly and said: "When did you come back Mashdi Hassan?"

"I came right now," Mashdi Hassan said, "The bitch hasn't given water to the cow, God's creature is dying out of thirst."

Islam left the cart and came toward Mashdi Hassan and asked: "She hasn't given water to the cow?"

"Of course she hasn't, the tongueless animal is dying." Mashdi Hassan said.

"Have you seen the cow?" Islam said.

"No, I haven't," Mashdi Hassan said, "But I know what in what mood she must be."

"But, didn't she tell you?" Islam said.

Mashdi Hassan filled the bucket with water from the pool and said: "She didn't tell me what?"

Islam coughed and said: "Because, Ismail's gone to track it."

"Ismail's gone to track what?" Mashdi Hassan said.

And he started walking toward his house in hurry. Islam, as he was walking shoulder to shoulder with Mashdi Hassan, said: "After the cow, didn't she tell you that she ran away last night?"

Mashdi Hassan stopped and said: "Who's run away?"

"It's nothing serious. Sure she's just around here. They'll find her anyway." Islam said.

"Who's run away, Ismail?" Mashdi Hassan said.

"No," Islam said, "The cow, your cow's run away."

Mashdi Hassan started running. While the water kept waving from the edge of the bucket and sprinkling on his legs and trousers legs, and he was ceaselessly shouting: "It's a lie, the cow hasn't run away, my cow doesn't run away."

And Islam said: "They'll find her, they've found her, right tonight, he'll bring her right tonight Mashdi Hassan."

They stopped when they reached the stable. Mashdi Hassan put the bucket of water down and sank in thoughts for some moments and then rubbed his hand against the damp legs of his trousers and opened the door of the stable with closed eyes and smelled and said: "She hasn't run away, my cow hasn't run away. She's right here, she's right here!"

"Yeah Mashdi Hassan, Yeah," Islam said, "Don't be gloomy. The cow's not run away."

Mashdi Hassan turned his back to the stable door and said: "Yeah, she's right here, do you smell her? She's right here. Look Mashdi Islam, don't you want to give her this water? You know, it's a good deed."

Islam went forward and said: "Why not, why not, I'll give it to her."

He picked the bucket of water up and went in. Mashdi Hassan, as he was standing, didn't dare to turn and look at the stable. He heard Islam's footsteps which went to the front of the pen and he heard the cow that put her muzzle into the bucket and started drinking.

When Islam came out, Mashdi Hassan was standing just as before with his back to the door, crying with joy.

## 6

About the evening, Islam and the Headman and Mashdi Jabbar and Abbas and the Redhead came to the front of Mashdi Hassan's house; Papakh and Islam's black goat were moving before them. When Mashdi Hassan's wife saw the crowd, she ran to the threshold with bare feet.

"We've come to see Mashdi Hassan," Islam said, "Is he all right?"

Mashdi Hassan's wife came forward and signaled them to talk quietly.

"What's he doing?" Islam asked again.

"Nothing," Mashdi Hassan's wife said, "He says that his cow isn't lost, he says my cow wouldn't get lost, she doesn't run away, she's right here, you're lying to me."

"Hasn't he gone to the stable?" the Headman asked.

"No he hasn't," Mashdi Hassan's wife said, "There he is, sitting on the roof of the stable and staring at the desert, look at him."

The men looked at the roof of the stable and saw that Mashdi Hassan was crouched down on the roof of the stable, his back to them, with his arms around the knees.

"Ok, what shall we do now?" Islam said.

"Let's go talk to him." The Headman said.

"Yeah," Islam said, "Let's go and tell him that his cow isn't there."

"He's just been sitting there laughing and crying over and over again." Mashdi Hassan's wife said, "He says my cow is right here, you're lying."

Islam signaled to the Headman. The crowd entered the yard and all of them climbed the heap of dust by the stable. They raised their heads and lined against the ledge of the roof. When Mashdi Hassan turned and saw the heads at first he was scared and after looking at them for a good while, he slowly crept forward and sat with crossed legs and said: "What a bad man you are Islam. How long have you been bearing me a grudge? What's this that you've done to me?"

Then he turned and said to the Headman: "Headman, ask him if he bears me a grudge, but I have never done him any wrong. By the pool he told me that the cow's run away, I know he's lying, he wants to scare me, how can my cow run away? Where can she go if she runs away?"

"Yeah Mashdi Hassan!" the Headman said, "You know, Islam doesn't bear you a grudge. He's no one's enemy. He's right about that, your cow's run away; but, don't you ask where the cow is? Don't you ask where Mashdi Ismail is?"

"Mashdi Ismail's gone to look and find the cow." The Redhead said.

Mashdi Hassan's wife's sobbing rose who was standing in the yard.

Mashdi Hassan drew himself back in horror and said: "It's a lie, my cow's right here. My cow hasn't run away, I know her smell, she hasn't gone out of here."

"If your cow hasn't run away and is in the stable, why don't you go to her?" Islam said.

"Yeah," the Headman said, "Mashdi Islam is right, why don't you go to her?"

"Go to your cow Mashdi Hassan." The Redhead said.

"Go to it Mashdi Hassan." Abbas said.

"Yeah go. Why are you sitting here?" Mashdi Jabbar said.

Mashdi Hassan drew himself back more and sat on the other side of the roof-hole and said: "I'm not going down, I'll sit right here."

"Why won't you go down?" the Headman said.

"I'm afraid if I went down and …" Mashdi Hassan said.

Mashdi Jabbar interrupted him: "Saw the cow's not there…"

Mashdi Hassan loudly said: "No, no, the cow's there. I know, I know."

"So what are you sitting here for?" Abbas said.

Mashdi Hassan was baffled and said: "Nothing. I'm sitting here and looking at that, you see, it's coming up from Pooruss."

The line of the heads turned and saw the moon which was rising from Pooruss like an old kite.

Mashdi Hassan laughed and said: "Yeah, here I am. Go; go mind your own business. I'm waiting here for the moon to come up, so that I can go down and take some water for her."

The line of the heads went down from the ledge of the roof and Mashdi Hassan's wife's sobbing rose again from the yard.

## 7

All the night long the roaring of a tireless cow straying in the alleys of Bayal had made everyone sleepless.

Abbas and his sister and Ismail who was hiding in their house had put their heads out of the window and were looking at the pool and at a small, black shape moving hither and thither on the water and the other Bayalers were sitting on windowsills and were looking at the pool and at a big, black figure which was running in the alleys and imitating a cow's mowing.

When it was light, Mashdi Hassan who was sweating and roaring came running toward his house from the desert and ran straight to the stable and reached himself to the pen and gripped at the edge of the pen.

Mashdi Touba opened the window and went on the roof of the stable and from the roof-hole, she saw that Mashdi Hassan has sunk his head into the pen, is stamping his feet on earth, and is roaring. Just like their cow's roaring at those times when Mashdi Hassan was going to take it to the desert.

## 8

Islam and the Headman and Mashdi Jabbar and Abbas and the Redhead and, after them, Papakh, came to Mashdi Hassan's house. When Mashdi Hassan's wife saw the crowd she half-opened the door and said: "He's come and gone to the stable, he's making noises like a cow's."

"May God himself have mercy." The Headman said.

"Let's go and see what he is doing." Abbas said.

"He has the right to do so," Islam said, "He has the right to do anything he does, it's all over for him now, he's lost."

Mashdi Hassan's wife started crying. The men went and gathered in front of the hatch of the stable and looked at

Mashdi Hassan who was standing over the well and had sunk his head into the pen and was stamping his feet on earth.

"Mashdi, Mashdi Hassan," the Headman said, "look, see what I'm saying."

"Look, Mashdi," Abbas said, "The Headman says that your cow is found."

"Tell him bit by bit," Islam said, "Don't tell him at once, can't you see that he's out of his senses?"

"Mashdi Hassan," Abbas said, "The Headman says that Ismail is back and he's found the cow and has brought it back."

Mashdi Hassan took his head out of the pen. His face was blood-stained and his tired, upset eyes were turning in the sockets. His mouth was full of grass that he was chewing; he looked at the men, grumbled in the throat and put his head into the pen again.

"No use talking to him this way." Abbas said.

"He's sort of changed, isn't he Mashdi Islam?" Mashdi Jabbar said.

"Why is he acting like that Mashdi Islam?" the Headman coughed and said.

Islam sank in thoughts and said: "I'm afraid Mashdi Hassan wastes away. He's really becoming a cow."

The Redhead was afraid and moved backwards and said: "A cow?"

"Yeah, a cow!" Islam said.

"What shall we do?" the Headman said.

"What shall we do?" Islam said, "Let's go in. Maybe we can do something for him."

Abbas turned to the Redhead and said: "Don't be afraid son, he's not a cow, he's Mashdi Hassan, he's our own Mashdi Hassan, come on, come on in!"

Islam opened the door of the stable. The men entered one by one. Mashdi Hassan's wife went on the roof. She sat down and, from the roof-hole, stared at the men who were all sitting by the mast, opposite to Mashdi Hassan.

## 9

Abbas' sister was sorting wheat grains and Ismail was sitting in front of the window and he was looking at his sister's house and was waiting for the men to return.

"Do you think he'll get well again?" Abbas' sister said.

"God knows," Ismail said, "But I know that Mashdi Hassan loves his cow far more than he loves my sister."

"All Bayalers are like that." Abbas' sister said.

"I can get up and go now," Ismail said, "Mashdi Hassan wouldn't come out to look and find me anyway?"

"I'm cooking porridge now," Abbas' sister said, "Eat and then go."

"Won't you let me go if I don't eat porridge?" Ismail said.

"Eat your porridge so that I let you go." Abbas' sister said.

Ismail laughed and said nothing. Abbas' sister said nothing either. When she finished sorting the wheat grains and rose to go she asked: "Mashdi Ismail, when are you going to take a wife? You know, your hair is a good deal white."

"Wait till Mashdi Hassan gets well," Ismail said, "Then I'll send my sister to suit you for me."

Abbas' sister's face turned red and she laughed and said: "You like porridge? Don't you? What about eggs?"

## 10

Mashdi Hassan turned and looked at the men who were sitting before the mast from one end to the other. Crushed fodder was hanging from his lips.

Islam coughed and, minding his tongue, said: "Mashdi Hassan, Hello, we've come to see if you feel well? How are you?"

Mashdi Hassan, chewing the cud, said: "I'm not Mashdi Hassan. I'm a cow. I am Mashdi Hassan's cow."

The Redhead was afraid and drew back.

"Don't talk like that Mashdi Hassan," the Headman said, "You are the very Mashdi Hassan himself, aren't you?"

Mashdi Hassan stamped his foot on earth and said: "No, I am not. I am Mashdi Hassan's cow!"

"Mashdi Hassan, don't say that," Mashdi Jabbar said, "If the Poorussians know, they'll come and steal you."

Abbas and the Headman laughed, Islam gave him a nasty look, the Redhead drew himself back and hid behind Islam.

Mashdi Hassan chewed the cud and said: "No, no, the Poorussians can't come here, Mashdi Hassan is sitting up there on the roof and he is looking after me."

"Mashdi Hassan, for God's sake, stop it," the Headman said, "What is this trouble that you've made for Bayal? You're not a cow, you're Mashdi Hassan!"

Mashdi Hassan stamped his foot on earth and said: "No, I am not Mashdi Hassan; Mashdi Hassan has gone to Seyedabad to labor. I am Mashdi Hassan's cow."

"There's no God but Allah," the Headman said, "But, what kind of cow are you? What do you have from cowness? But, where's your tail?"

"Aha," Mashdi Jabbar said, "Where's your tail? Where's your hoof?"

Mashdi Hassan suddenly jumped, as he was running madly around the stable and striding and once in every several steps he knocked his head against the wall and roared; he stopped when he was in front of the pen.

His chest rose and fell for some moments. Then he put his head in the pen and filled his mouth with grass and came and stood over the well. The very spot on which Islam had strewn straw, and with a voice which came out of his throat with trouble he said: "Can't I be a cow without a tail, without a hoof? Won't you accept me without a tail?"

And he started trampling on the earth.

"Listen, you Mashdi Hassan's cow," Islam said, "Yesterday before the dawn, Mashdi Hassan's wife came to the side of the pool and cried that Mashdi Hassan's cow was dead, I and the Headman and Ismail and this kid came, and dug under your very feet, just where you're standing, and threw Mashdi Hassan's cow there. If you're Mashdi Hassan's cow you must be in that well, and if you're not, so you're Mashdi Hassan himself. Am I right?"

Mashdi Hassan started running around the stable again. This time faster and more angrily, he spat everything he had in his mouth out and began roaring: "Oh, Mashdi Hassan, oh, Mashdi Hassan. Hey, hey Mashdi Hassan, come here, the Poorussians have rushed in here and want to steal me, they want to take me to Pooruss. They want to cut my head off and throw me into a well, hey Mashdi Hassan! Hey, Mashdi Hassan!"

The men stood up.

"Ok, ok, Mashdi Hassan's cow," Islam said, "we're leaving now. We're not Poorussians. I'm Islam and this is the Headman and these two are Abbas and Mashdi Jabbar. And you know this kid too, we're going. Sleep in your stable. Is there anything you like me to bring for you?"

Mashdi Hassan was calm and happy and he started chewing the cud slowly and said: "Bring me grass, bring me alfalfa, bring me straw, bring me water, water!"

And he started roaring, a roar that a thirsty cow can let out.

## 11

When it was past midnight, three Poorussians came out of the village. With the ropes that they had hung on their shoulders and the daggers that they had on their waists.

"Where shall we go?" the first Poorussian said.

"Let's go to Bayal." The second Poorussian said.

"Yeah, let's go there. Let's go to Bayal." The third Poorussian said.

"Go there for what? We can't get anything in Bayal." The first Poorussian said.

"Today in Khatoonabad they said that Mashdi Hassan's cow is dead." The second Poorussian said.

"What can we do with it?" The first Poorussian said.

"We go and skin it." The second Poorussian said.

"Haven't they skinned it themselves?" The first Poorussian said.

"In Khatoonabad, they said that they've thrown it away without skinning it." The second Poorussian said.

"Let's go then. Before a beast gets it, let's get ourselves there." The first Poorussian said.

"Let's go seek and find it." The second Poorussian said.

"By the way, someone told me in "Jamishan" that the cow is still in the stable." The third Poorussian said.

"So much the better, let's move." The first Poorussian said.

"Let's go!" the second and the third Poorussian said together.

The three men with the ropes and daggers started for Bayal from the by-way.

## 12

When the Poorussians reached Bayal, it was totally dark. They drew the daggers and crept into the village by the Landlord's garden. Papakh which was sleeping on the wall of the garden raised his head and as soon as he saw the black figures, let out a loud howl and jumped down and ran to the front of Islam's house and scratched the earth.

Islam, who was sleepless, was looking at the neighbor's house from the hole in the closet. He rose and came to the window; Papakh shook his tail and became silent. Islam heard the Poorussians' rustling and drew himself aside and hid behind the windowsill. Mashdi Safar put his head out of the roof-hole and watched the pool. Abbas' sister and Ismail, who were hiding behind a wall, craned. The Poorussians were approaching like three dark phantoms from the pool.

"Do you see?" Ismail said.

"Who are they?" Abbas' sister softly asked.

Ismail swallowed his spittle and said: "Poorussians, Poorussians!"

Abbas' sister asked with fear: "Poorussians?"

And she was going to scream when Ismail put his hand over her mouth, then Abbas' sister, bent down, ran by the rim of the wall and went to their house and shook Abbas who was sleeping by the window and said: "Abbas, Abbas, the Poorussians have rushed into the village."

Abbas got up and looked. The Poorussians took the turn into the alley. When Abbas and Ismail reached the alley with sticks in their hands, Islam and Mashdi Safar's son were also approaching on tiptoe with clubs in their hands. Mashdi Jabbar and Mashdi Baba also appeared. The Bayalers moved.

The Poorussians approached Mashdi Hassan's house with daggers in their hands and stopped there.

"There's a rumble." The first Poorussian said.

"Yeah," The second Poorussian said, "It's the noise of a cow's panting."

"So the cow's alive." The third Poorussian said.

"Undo the ropes," The first Poorussian said, "We'll tie its mouth and pull it out."

The second and the third Poorussian undid the ropes.

"You two go in," The first Poorussian said, "I'll be on watch here."

He held his dagger tightly and stood there. As the second and the third Poorussian turned to look back they saw the Bayalers lined behind their backs with sticks in their hands. The Poorussians were moved, and they stood still in their places. The first Poorussian, dagger in his hand, also turned and stood still.

Mashdi Hassan's wife who was sleeping on the roof of the stable woke and sat up. Mashdi Hassan started groaning from within the stable. The Bayalers attacked with sticks in their hands. The Poorussians jumped on the heap of dust behind the stable and to Mashdi Hassan's roof from there and before the Bayalers could arrive, dropped the ropes and raised the daggers.

"Don't let them run away." Islam shouted.

The men attacked with a roar. Mashdi Hassan's wife screamed out of horror. Before the men could reach the roof, the Poorussians threw themselves into the Landlord's garden and when the Bayalers were by the wall the Poorussians were lost in the byway from the outskirt of Bayal like the wind.

The Headman came out with a lantern and saw the men on the roofs with sticks in their hands. He came hurriedly and when he saw Islam he quickly asked: "What's up? What's happened Mashdi Islam?"

"Nothing," Islam said, "Nothing, the Poorussians had come to steal Mashdi Hassan."

## 13

When the sun rose, Islam appeared from behind the Landlord's garden with the cart full of alfalfa and came to the side of the pool. Abbas' sister was sitting by the black stone for washing the dead and was washing dishes. A gentle wind was blowing and shaking the leaves of alfalfa.

Islam took the bucket out from under the cart and filled it with water from the pool and held it before the horse's muzzle. The horse started drinking water.

Islam's black goat put its head out of the window and took a look and went in again. Islam hung the bucket under the cart and then climbed the wheel and took an armful of fresh alfalfa which he had wrapped in a sack and came down. He passed the first alley and reached Mashdi Hassan's house. Mashdi Hassan's wife was sitting on the roof of the stable and had covered her face and fallen asleep.

Islam pushed the hatch of the stable aside and poured the alfalfa in and returned. Mashdi Baba's coughing, who had newly woke up, could be heard from afar.

## 14

When the sun set, Islam appeared from behind the Landlord's garden with the empty cart and came to the side of the pool. The women were sitting opposite to Baba Ali's house and Mashdi Safar's son was pulling the carcass of a chicken out of the pool with a long stick. Islam took the cart to the front of his house. The black goat came out and first looked at Islam and then at the cart and went to the horse. The horse brought its head down and closed its eyes. Islam took the empty bucket off the hook under the cart and went to the edge of the pool, he filled the bucket. He passed the first alley and reached Mashdi Hassan's house. Mashdi Hassan's wife was sitting on the roof of the stable and had covered her face and fallen asleep.

Islam pushed the door of the stable aside and went in. A gentle, cold wind was blowing and taking a tired cow's groaning out with itself.

## 15

Islam and the Headman and Mashdi Jabbar and Abbas and Ismail and the Redhead were sitting by the stone lion in the graveyard.

"Now, what shall we do with him?" the Headman said.

"We have to do something with him." Abbas said.

"And he doesn't even talk anymore." Mashdi Jabbar said.

"And when you talk to him, he makes noises like a cow's." Islam said.

"He's learnt the language of cows so quickly." The Redhead said.

The Headman gave him a nasty look. The Redhead became silent and drew back.

"And he eats alfalfa and grass ceaselessly." Mashdi Jabbar said.

"I'm afraid that he gets his guts wounded." Ismail said.

The Headman coughed and said: "What shall we do Mashdi Islam?"

"Let's take him to the city." Islam said.

"To do what?" Ismail said.

"We must take him to the hospital," Islam said, "Anyway, we hadn't the power. Maybe they can bring home to him that he's himself and hasn't become a cow."

"By what shall we take him?" the Headman said.

"By my cart." Islam said.

"He won't get on the cart," the Redhead said, "You can't get a cow on a cart unless you behead it."

Islam turned and said to the Redhead: "If he doesn't get on the cart then we'll take him on foot."

"Now, suppose that we took him to the city and they didn't accept him at the hospital, what shall we do then?" Mashdi Jabbar said.

Ismail laughed and said: "He's right, what if they said they didn't accept cows?"

"Mashdi Islam knows better," the Headman said, "we must do whatever Mashdi Islam says."

Mashdi Jabbar coughed and said: "We'll bring him back here if they didn't accept him."

"What do you say Mashdi Islam?" the Headman said.

"Yeah," Islam said, "The three of us will take him to the city."

"Which three?" the Headman said.

"The three who can handle him." Ismail said.

"Mashdi Baba doesn't like him, he wouldn't come." Islam said.

"Let Mashdi Baba come not." The Headman said.

"Tell those who will come." Abbas said.

"I and the Headman and Mashdi Jabbar," Islam said, "The three of us will take him."

The Headman thought and then said: "As for me, I'm coming. What about you Mashdi Jabbar? Are you coming too?"

"Of course I'm coming," Mashdi Jabbar said, "And Mashdi Hassan's wife can come to my house so that my spouse wouldn't be left alone."

"He's right," Abbas said, "One shouldn't leave a newly-wed bride alone."

"So it's settled." The Headman said.

"Now, let's get up and go and find three ropes," Islam said, "When it gets dark, we'll go for him."

"All right", the Headman said, "We'll be in front of the stable when it's dark."

Mashdi Jabbar coughed and rose. The others also rose. The sun hadn't gone away yet, and it was a lot of time left for darkness to come.

## 16

When it was dark, three men from Bayal came out of their houses. With the ropes they were carrying on their shoulders and the bundles of bread they had under their arms.

When they reached the front of Mashdi Hassan's house, they found each other in the darkness.

"You came?" Islam said.

"Yeah, I came." The Headman said.

"I came too." Mashdi Jabbar said.

Islam turned and said to Mashdi Jabbar: "You told his wife?"

"Yeah," Mashdi Jabbar said, "I told; and it was agreed that as soon as we took Mashdi Hassan, his wife would go to my house."

"So everything is settled, isn't it?" Islam said.

Mashdi Hassan's wife opened the window and came on the roof of the stable and brought a lighted lantern with her.

"We're taking Mashdi." The Headman said.

Mashdi Hassan's wife started crying and kneeled on the roof.
"Let's get in." Islam said.

Mashdi Jabbar opened the door of the stable. The three of them went in carefully. Mashdi Hassan's wife, sitting just as she was, hung the lantern down from the roof-hole. In the light of the lantern the men saw Mashdi Hassan who had fallen asleep in front of the pen.

## 17

At the bottom of the valley, in the darkness, three men were dragging a cow whom they had tied with ropes toward the road. One of them was walking in the front and pulling the rope and the other two were pushing him. The cow, with his small figure, would resist and tire the men.

Three men from Pooruss, with daggers on their waists, had bent down from the peak of a mountain and were watching them.

## 18

About the evening, Islam and the Headman and Mashdi Jabbar returned to Bayal. The sound of tambourine and kettle-drum was in the air from the village.

The men were sitting beside the pool and smoking pipes. Mashdi Baba, as soon as he saw them, rose and came and said to Islam: "Where are you Mashdi Islam? Run, run and get your instrument and come and go to Abbas' house."

"Get my instrument and go to Abbas' house to do what?" Islam said.

"It's Mashdi Ismail's wedding," Mashdi Baba said, "He's married Abbas' sister."

"I've got work to do. I've got a lot of work to do. I feel sleepy." Islam said.

Mashdi Baba asked in wonder: "What? You don't want to play the instrument? You know that it brings good luck for the bride and the groom?"

"I know," Islam said, "But I won't play the instrument."

Mashdi Baba followed Islam for several steps and then turned and looked back. The Headman and Mashdi Jabbar parted and went to their houses.

Mashdi Baba said: "Hey, Mashdi Islam, what news from Mashdi Hassan?"

Islam said: "Mashdi Hassan? Before reaching the city…"

He cut what he was saying and went to his house and lied down and stared at the neighbor's roof from the hatch in the closet.

Islam's black goat came out of the closet, looked at Islam and went out by the window.

Papakh which was sitting under the willow, rose and, with Islam's goat, passed from among the crowd and went to the first alley that was empty and quiet. Only the sound of Mashdi Hassan's wife's crying, who was sitting all alone on the roof of the stable with her lighted lantern, could be heard, and the sound of clapping and drums that were getting closer and faster little by little, and the helpless roaring of an unknown cow from within a ruined stable.

# Fifth Story

## 1

It was a good while past noon when Abbas said goodbye to Sattar and Mashdi Rahim and Mir-Hamzeh and came out of Khatoonabad. The sunshine was spread over the wheat and Abbas who didn't want the sunshine to fall into his eyes, was looking before his feet and striding toward Bayal. When he walked for about a hundred steps, he felt that someone was following him, slowly and panting. "Who's this that's following me?" Abbas thought.

He stopped and turned suddenly; he saw a big hairy dog standing behind him with opened mouth and looking at him with kind eyes and shaking its tail.

Abbas jerked the stick he had in his hand and shouted: "Shoo! Shoo!"

The dog turned and looked at Khatoonabad and shook its tail again. Abbas moved forward. Some handfuls of the dog's hair were missing and a big scar was on its neck. Being so old, it still had firm, healthy teeth and was looking at him with big, shiny eyes.

Abbas took the dog's ear and turned its head toward Khatoonabad and gently stroke its back with the stick he had in his hand and said: "Shoo! Shoo!"

And he started walking. When he moved about a hundred steps, he turned and looked again; the hairy one was slowly following him. Abbas stopped. The dog also stopped. Abbas jerked his stick and shouted: "Shoo! Shoo! Shoo!"

The dog turned and took several steps backward and sat and looked at Abbas. "Huh, you tongueless beast, what's wrong with you?" Abbas said.

## Fifth Story

The dog moved forward and sat down. "Come on, now that you're so cheeky, come on." Abbas said.

The dog came running and shook its tail and stood several steps away from Abbas, it first looked at him carefully. When Abbas smiled, the dog put its muzzle on earth and shook its tail quickly and raised dust.

Abbas moved forward and put his foot gently on the dog's head and said: "What do you want? Huh? Be not afraid, tell me! What do you want?"

The dog closed its eyes and grumbled. Abbas said: "Why do you behave like that, you dying beast?"

The dog whipped the earth with its tail again.

From behind the garden wall, a Khatoonabadian's head appeared and looked at the dog and Abbas and laughed.

"Whose dog is this dying bear?" Abbas said.

"It's no one's." the Khatoonabadian said.

"So, why does it behave like that? What's wrong with it?" Abbas said.

The Khatoonabadian laughed and said: "It's looking for an owner. It's been a year and some months since Mir-Hamzeh has abandoned it. And the miserable beast is tired of roving and wants to bind itself to someone."

Abbas took the dog's head with both hands and asked: "Why has Mir-Hamzeh abandoned it?"

"When it got wounded and couldn't run well anymore, then Mir-Hamzeh abandoned it." The Khatoonabadian said.

"How come it got wounded?" Abbas said.

"One night some Poorusslans had come to Khatoonabad and were hanging around here and Mir-Hamzeh sent it to catch them." The Khatoonabadian said, "And they were kind enough to tear its neck off with daggers and knives and then they ran away."

"And then Mir-Hamzeh threw it out?" Abbas said.

"Yeah," the Khatoonabadian said, "And nobody has owned it since then."

The dog had stretched on earth and put its muzzle in the dust and had raised its eyelids. It was watching Abbas who was in thoughts and fancies.

"Take it if you like," the Khatoonabadian said, "To Bayal."

"Take it to do what with?" Abbas said.

"Take and keep it." The Khatoonabadian said.

"I'm afraid the dogs of Bayal won't let it in." Abbas said.

"The dogs *will* let it in." the Khatoonabadian said, "If the people didn't let it in abandon it, then it'll come back to Khatoonabad by itself."

He laughed and ducked his head. Abbas moved, the dog also rose and moved. Abbas stopped and shouted: "Shoo! Shoo! Shoo!"

The dog put its muzzle on earth and groaned. Abbas said: "Get up, get up and come, you cheeky one."

They started moving side by side. When they reached "Shoor", it was almost evening. Abbas sat on a large boulder and opened his kerchief to have something to eat. And the Khatoonabadian dog went and sat on a height and gazed at Bayal.

## 2

When they were near Bayal, the Khatoonabadian stopped and looked at his opposite carefully. It drew itself behind Abbas and hid there. "What's wrong with you poor beast?" Abbas said.

Papakh's panting was heard who was coming from the opposite side. Abbas said: "Don't be afraid, it isn't a stranger, it's Papakh, and he won't hurt you."

Both of them stood and waited. Papakh came and stopped at several steps from Abbas and looked at Abbas and the Khatoonabadian with wonder.

"Don't be afraid, this newcomer will never hurt you. Move, both of you, come on, Shoo! Shoo!"

Papakh turned and ran toward Bayal quickly. Abbas and the Khatoonabadian started walking side by side. When they reached Bayal, the sun had set. The dogs of Bayal were lined on the Landlord's garden wall and Papakh was in front of all of them. When the Khatoonabadian saw the line of dogs sitting from one end to the other, it stopped and looked at them in fear.

"Come on," Abbas said, "They won't hurt you."

The Khatoonabadian entered the village by Abbas' side. When they were at the head of the alley, Islam's black goat came forward and looked at the newcomer carefully. Abbas and the Khatoonabadian went to the side of the pool and reached in front of Baba Ali's house where the men were gathered together and were chatting.

When Mashdi Baba who was sitting on a heap of firewood saw Abbas he said: "Mashdi Abbas is back."

The men turned and looked at him.

"Look at the other one." Mashdi Jabbar said.

"Look at the dog, look at the dog!" the Redhead said.

Ismail rose, came forward and said: "Where have you got this Abbas?"

Abbas went to the men. The Khatoonabadian also went. "I've brought this from Khatoonabad." Abbas said.

"Was there a lack of bread-consumers in Bayal that you brought another one too?" Abdullah said.

"It didn't let me alone," Abbas said, "No matter what I did, it didn't let me alone at all and followed me."

Mashdi Baba bent down and looked at the Khatoonabadian's eyes and said: "Isn't it the one to which last year the Poorussians gave a good piece of their mind?"

"Yeah, that's it." Abbas said.

"It was Mir-Hamzeh's, wasn't it?" Mashdi Baba said.

"Yeah, that's it." Abbas said.

"You've brought it in vain. It's of no use to anyone." Mashdi Baba said.

"Will you let it loose in the village?" Abdullah said.

"No, I'm taking it to my house." Abbas said.

Baba Ali brought his head out of the hatch in the enclosure and said: "If you had brought a woman from Khatoonabad with you instead of this carcass, it would be of more use to you."

"Abbas is shy," Mashdi Baba said, "His aunt must do it. He himself can only go and snatch old, worn-out dogs from Khatoonabad and bring them to Bayal."

"Good," the Redhead said, "We'll take it to the graveyard at nights to take care of the dead."

"Hey kid! Don't you get mixed with men." Mashdi Jabbar said.

"And don't be too funny either!" Ismail said.

The Redhead was embarrassed and went to the back of the firewood.

"You brought this half-dead beast here in vain Abbas." Abdullah said.

"Yeah, you brought it in vain." Mashdi Baba said.

"But it's not a sin, is it? If I couldn't keep it, I'll take it back to Khatoonabad." Abbas said.

"And besides, do you think that Papakh and the other dogs will let it stay in Bayal?" Mashdi Jabbar said.

"They won't hurt him," Abbas said, "If you allow."

"Be not so sure, they'll skin it in a few days." Ismail said.

The Headman who had newly arrived came and sat on the firewood and said: "What kind of gift is this that you've brought with you Abbas?"

Abbas crouched beside the men and said: "This unfortunate beast hasn't got a good owner, it's sticking to me and wouldn't let go."

Baba Ali brought his head out of the hatch and said: "Headman, it's all because of being unsettled. It's better to raise arms and settle a marriage for Abbas. Perhaps he'll be entertained."

"May God will," the Headman said, "We'll raise arms in winter and settle a real marriage."

And he stared at the dog and said: "Isn't it Mir-Hamzeh's?"

"Yeah, that's it." Abbas said.

Mashdi Safar's son came and sat beside the Headman. The Headman said: "The tongueless beast has grown old, and too old too."

"But his teeth are healthy, do you see?" Abbas said.

He held up the dog's muzzle and opened its lips and showed its teeth.

"But teeth are no reason for being young," Mashdi Safar's son said, "Mashdi Baba's got teeth too, open your mouth Mashdi Baba! Open it, look."

He took Mashdi Baba's chin and opened his lips. The Redhead laughed loudly from behind the firewood.

"Abbas, it's better to send it back to Khatoonabad with a flock right now." The Headman said.

"He's right Abbas, we don't feel like seeing it." Mashdi Jabbar said.

"Seems like it's become a little loony too, the way it looks at you!" the Headman said.

"It's obvious," Mashdi Jabbar said, "If it had good sense, Mir-Hamzeh wouldn't throw it out."

"I suppose it can do nothing but sleeping." The Headman said.

"Well, it has no more strength." Mashdi Jabbar said.

"All these things apart, then auntie won't let you take it into the house." Ismail said.

"Oh yeah, how can she let an unclean dog in her house?" the Headman said.

"Which of you takes his dog *in* his house that you think I would do it?" Abbas said.

And he rose. The men also rose and started walking toward outside the village. When they were by the valley, Mashdi Safar's son said: "Give it a hard kick on the head and make short work of it."

"Why should I do that?" Abbas said, "Kick the tongueless beast for no reason?"

And he took the Khatoonabadian's ear and took it several steps forward and held it facing Khatoonabad and said: "Shoo! Shoo! Shoo!"

The dog took several steps and stopped.

"Shoo!" Abbas shouted.

"So cheeky!" Mashdi Jabbar said.

"It can be put an end to with a kick." Mashdi Safar's son said.

"It's a sin," the Headman said, "Why should he kick the tongueless beast?"

It was dark and the Khatoonabadian was standing in a distance of a hundred steps and was looking at the men when Islam appeared.

"You're late Mashdi Islam?" the Headman said.

"What's happened that you're all gathered here?" Islam said.

"Abbas has gone to Khatoonabad and brought an old, dying dog with him and now we have a mind to throw it out." The Headman said.

Islam came forward and bent down and looked at the Khatoonabadian and said: "He's not that much old. What a good way of looking at you he has, and his teeth are healthy too."

Mashdi Baba and Mashdi Jabbar and the Redhead and Mashdi Safar's son suddenly rose and jumped forward and roared: "Shoo! Shoo!"

The Khatoonabadian threw itself into the darkness with horror and the Bayalers burst into laughter.

## 3

Abbas woke up before the dawn; the aunt had gone out to the side of the pool to wash dishes. Abbas took his lunch bundle and came out. Islam had also come out and was fixing his cart.

"You've got up so early Mashdi Islam?" Abbas said.

"I couldn't sleep till morning." Islam said.

"Why couldn't you sleep?" Abbas said.

"The dogs kept bow-wowing till the morning and didn't let me sleep." Islam said.

"Was something up?" Abbas said.

"No," Islam said, "I came two or three times and looked all around the village. Nothing was up. The dogs were sitting in a line upon the Landlord's garden wall, facing the desert and were bow-wowing."

"As for me, I didn't wake up," Abbas said, "I was too tired and I was sleeping like a log."

"Good for you." Islam said.

Abbas moved on and went toward the desert. When he came out of Bayal, the sun rose and the white hills around "Shoor" lighted up. Abbas fixed his eyes down and walked. When he walked for about a hundred steps, he felt that someone was following him, slowly and panting. "Who's this that's following me?" Abbas thought.

He stopped and thought and turned. The Khatoonabadian was standing behind his back, it was looking at him with kind, afraid eyes and shaking its tail.

Abbas stopped and said: "You haven't gone yet, and you are waiting for me?"

The Khatoonabadian shook its tail and brought its muzzle toward the earth.

Abbas moved forward and grabbed the Khatoonabadian by the ears and held its head up and looked in its eyes. The Khatoonabadian whipped the earth with its hairy tail and raised dust.

"What do you want?" Abbas said, "What do you want, huh? You don't want to go back? You want to stay with me? I think you like me and Bayal."

The Khatoonabadian put its head on earth and licked Abbas's feet.

"Get up," Abbas said, "Get up and let's go to work, it's getting too late."

Both of them, shoulder to shoulder with each other, moved toward the desert with long steps.

## 4

About the evening, they came to Bayal. When they were near the Landlord's garden, the Khatoonabadian stopped and looked at his opposite with fear.

"Move, old man!" Abbas said.

Papakh's panting was heard who came from the opposite and stopped. "Don't panic," Abbas said, "Come on, never mind him!"

Papakh went back running into the village. When Abbas and the Khatoonabadian reached the side of the pool, the dogs of Bayal came to the front of Islam's house and watched the newcomer.

"Don't go in a fighting mood," Abbas said, "Come on, let's go. It's no time for a fight."

In front of Baba Ali's house, the men were sitting on the firewood, smoking pipes and chatting.

"Abbas," Mashdi Baba said, "You've brought this poor wretch here again."

"Couldn't you part with it?" Mashdi Jabbar said.

"Abbas likes it too much, Abbas likes old dogs too much." The Redhead said.

"But, what do you want to do with it?" Ismail said.

Abbas went forward and said: "I'll take him to my house and I'll keep him."

"Now that you like it, take it to your house and keep it." Mashdi Baba said.

"Seems that you yourself like owning a dying dog too Mashdi Baba!" Abdullah said.

"Abbas would happily give this carcass to you, if you like." Ismail said.

Abbas was excited and said: "No, I won't give him to anybody."

"Won't you even give it to me?" Mashdi Jabbar said.

"I won't even give him to you." Abbas said.

"What about me?" Abdullah said.

"Nobody, I won't give him to anybody." Abbas said.

"You wouldn't give it to me either?" Ismail said.

"Yeah, I won't give him to you either." Abbas said.

The Headman, who had newly arrived, said: "What's up? Is there a fight going on here?"

Baba Ali put his head out of the hatch and said: "Headman, Abbas has rated the Khatoonabadian too high, he wants to make a business by doing so."

The Redhead went behind the firewood and started laughing.

"Don't listen to anybody Abbas," the Headman said, "Now that you like it, take it to your house."

"What are you talking about Headman?" Ismail said, "Tell him to send it out, to throw it out of Bayal."

"Now I won't listen to anybody anymore. I'll listen to nobody." Abbas said.

Baba Ali put his head out of the hatch again and said: "Didn't I tell you Headman? Didn't I tell you Mashdi Baba, that he must be looked after?"

Abbas returned to the Khatoonabadian which was standing with his back to the men and the dogs of Bayal which had come to the side of the black stone for washing the dead and were looking at it kindly.

## 5

Abbas's aunt who had raised smoke behind a ruined wall and was cooking porridge, raised her head and looked in surprise and shouted: "What are you doing Abbas? Where are you bringing it?"

And she hastily made for the other side of the wall. She had a large, wooden spoon in her hand with which she had stirred the porridge.

"It's nothing," Abbas said, "This Khatoonabadian, I have bought him."

"What?" the aunt said, "You have bought it? You've paid money and bought this deformed thing?"

"No, I didn't buy it." Abbas said, "Mir-Hamzeh owed me something, for which he gave me this."

"And you accepted it?" the aunt said.

"No, I didn't accept him," Abbas said, "I just liked him; I liked him too much, in fact."

"Throw it out," the Aunt said, "Throw it out, let it go away."

"Throw him out?" Abbas said.

"Yeah, yeah, throw it out." The aunt said.

"I'll never throw him out." Abbas said.

"Then I'll go back to Hazavan to stay with my son." The aunt said.

"Go back to Hazavan? Do you think I'll ever let it happen?" Abbas said.

"It's either me or this beast." the aunt said.

"Don't be angry auntie, this poor wretch isn't here to take your place." Abbas said.

"It all depends on you now, go think about it." The aunt said.

Abbas and the Khatoonabadian went to the yard and the aunt returned to the other side of the wall. She put a new log into the fireplace and a huge amount of thick smoke rose in the shape of a column and went up.

# 6

In the morning, before the dawn, Abbas and the Khatoonabadian were going toward the desert when Mashdi Safar's son appeared on their way out of the blue and said to Abbas: "Going to the desert?"

"Yeah, I'm going to the desert." Abbas said.

"And not alone, you've found a comrade for yourself." Mashdi Safar's son said.

"Yeah, he's better than many men." Abbas said.

"You're right, and how much he looks like yourself." Mashdi Safar's son said.

"Right," Abbas said, "Thank God he doesn't look like you, then I had to smash his head with a stone and crush it and throw him into the valley."

"I want to tell you something Abbas." Mashdi Safar's son said.

"All right, tell it." Abbas said.

"I want to tell you not to make it so cheeky." Mashdi Safar's son said, "If it gets too cheeky, I and only I know what to do to it. I hate stranger dogs. And I hate them too much too."

"All right." Abbas said.

"Got it or not?" Mashdi Safar's son said.

"Yeah, I got it," Abbas said, "And I want to tell you something too. Go, go and tell Mashdi Safar to keep his son's mouth shut. If he gets too cheeky and mixes in people's business, there's someone in Bayal whose name is Abbas, he'll come and pluck his tongue out and throw it before a stranger dog which he has brought from Khatoonabad."

"All right." Mashdi Safar's son said.

"Got it or not?" Abbas said.

"Listen to what I'm telling you," Mashdi Safar's son said, "One week, I'll only give you a one-week respite to…"

Islam appeared riding the cart. He jumped down and said: "What's happened? What's up? Why are you staring at each other like that?"

"It's nothing Mashdi Islam." Abbas said.

Mashdi Safar's son laughed and said: "I was asking about his comrade's health and he got angry."

"Get on the cart, let's go." Islam said to Abbas.

Abbas got on the cart and sat beside Islam. Islam urged on the horse. The cart started moving and the Khatoonabadian after the cart, when they were taking the turn by the Landlord's garden the Khatoonabadian's howl rose. Abbas jumped down. A sharp stone had come and hit the Khatoonabadian's leg and Mashdi Safar's son was running quickly from the edge of the pool.

## 7

When Abbas and the Khatoonabadian came to Bayal, the aunt who had made fire and smoke behind the wall and was cooking porridge raised her head and saw Abbas and came to this side of the wall. She had a large, wooden spoon in her hand, with crushed grains of wheat on the spoon.

"You've brought this filth here again?" the aunt said.

"Yeah," Abbas said, "Was it agreed that I shouldn't bring him?"

"How many times have I told you to let it go?" the Aunt said.

"And I had told that I won't let him go." Abbas said.

"Then I'll go back to Hazavan to stay with my son." the Aunt said.

"Ok. Go any time you like." Abbas said.

"Do you know that you'll be miserable if I go and you, like Islam, must take care of yourself?" the Aunt said.

"There's no need for you to pity me and Islam." Abbas said.

"All right." the Aunt said.

"Now it all depends on you," Abbas said "Go if you like to or don't if you don't like to."

The aunt stood there and looked at him and went behind the wall and disappeared and a thick, dark-colored smoke rose in shape of a column and went up. Abbas and the Khatoonabadian went toward Islam's house. Abbas opened the window and went in. He took the enameled bowl and the bag and came to the edge of the pool. He rolled his sleeves up and started washing the Khatoonabadian.

First Papakh, and then Islam's black goat and at last the other dogs of Bayal and Mashdi Safar's son came and stood shoulder to shoulder with each other to watch Abbas and the Khatoonabadian which was shaking in vain and licking itself.

## 8

The men had gathered at the little square at the back of Mashdi Safar's house, sitting on the firewood and chatting.

"What do you think we shall do to him now?" Mashdi Jabbar said.

"Yeah," Mashdi Baba said, "from now on, we must have a good thought about it."

"He's changing more and more everyday." Abdullah said.

"Now that the weather's become hot, he wouldn't take it to the desert with himself." Mashdi Jabbar said.

"Why, does he go to the desert himself to take that filthy thing with him too?" Mashdi Baba said.

"Bayal must get rid of this bloody Khatoonabadian by any means." Abdullah said.

Uncle Zeinal who had come with help of crutches and was sitting by the heap of firewood said: "Let's go tell him to let it go."

The Redhead started laughing from behind the heap of firewood.

"He won't let it go," Mashdi Jabbar said, "We must think of another way."

"We could buy it from him if he would sell it." Abdullah said.

"No one would throw away a penny for this filthy thing." Mashdi Safar's son said.

Mashdi Jabbar turned his face to the Headman and said: "What do you say Headman?"

The Headman turned his face to Islam and said: "I don't know, I agree with whatever Mashdi Islam says."

Islam, who was frowning, said: "Let him be, now that Abbas is happy with an old dog, let him be happy."

Mashdi Jabbar and Mashdi Baba together said: "What? Let him be? Let him be happy?"

Mashdi Safar's son said to Mashdi Jabbar and Mashdi Baba: "Relax, I'll show you what we must do to it."

Islam rose and went away. And Uncle Zeinal, with the crutches, started walking and went toward the banner-house. It was the time for Adhan.[7] There was no sign of Adhan.

## 9

Abbas took the Khatoonabadian in the room and seated it before the window. The aunt had lighted a lamp and was sitting at the end of the room. Abbas took his dinner from the niche and came to the side of the window again. He ate half of the porridge and put the rest before the Khatoonabadian.

"I knew you would bring it into the house at last." The aunt said.

"I've washed it just now." Abbas said.

"Do you think dogs would become clean by washing?" the aunt said.

"All of you think that it'll become clean by killing." Abbas said.

When the dinner was over, Abbas and the Khatoonabadian went on the roof. When the aunt rose to go to bed, she raised her head out of the roof-hole and looked out. Abbas was

---

[7] The call to pray.

sleeping and the Khatoonabadian was sitting over Abbas's head, watching the stars and blinking from time to time.

## 10

Ismail and Mashdi Baba and Abdullah and Mashdi Jabbar and the Redhead and Mashdi Safar's son and Abbas's aunt were sitting at the little square at the back of Mashdi Safar's house beside the heap of firewood.

"Hey Abbas's aunt, how's Mashdi Abbas doing?" Mashdi Safar's son said to Abbas's aunt.

"Nothing," the aunt said, "He's abandoned all his works and is only after that bloody Khatoonabadian."

"And he doesn't go after any work either." Abdullah said.

"It's a long time he hasn't." the aunt said.

"He's ruining himself for the sake of a beast." Mashdi Baba said.

"What's it to us if he's ruining himself or not," Mashdi Safar's son said, "I hate that Khatoonabadian dog altogether. God knows that I even can't stand the sight of it."

"Neither do I." Mashdi Jabbar said.

"Think of unfortunate me who have to say prayers in that house." The aunt said.

"In every aspect it's both for the good of Abbas himself and for the good of Bayal that we get rid of this bloody thing." Ismail said.

"Today Abbas told me to go and take care of his dog in daytime." The Redhead said.

"He's going to find a manservant for a stray dog?" Mashdi Baba said.

"By God Abbas is out of his mind." Ismail said.

"He's been out of his mind from the first." Mashdi Safar's son said.

"All right, now tell us, what should we do?" Mashdi Jabbar said to Mashdi Safar's son.

Mashdi Safar's son crouched in the middle of the crowd and the others came closer, they were all ears.

"You must do the first job," Mashdi Safar's son said to Ismail.

Islam appeared riding the alfalfa-filled cart. He came and stopped opposite to the crowd and looked at them and said: "What are you going to do? Are you preparing a trick for Abbas's guest?"

Nobody answered Islam.

## 11

About the noon, Abbas had taken the Khatoonabadian to the edge of the pool and was washing it when Ismail appeared.

"What are you doing in the village at this time of the day Ismail?" Abbas asked.

"What are you doing yourself? Why haven't you gone to the field?" Ismail said.

"I wanted to wash and clean this poor animal." Abbas said.

"You've abandoned all of your works and just attend to this poor animal?" Ismail said.

"What shall I do?" Abbas said, "Who would attend to him if I don't? Auntie wouldn't, neither would the Headman, nor would Islam, nor would you, so who would attend to him?"

"All right," Ismail said, "You'll finish your job before the night, won't you?"

"Yeah, I'll finish it even earlier." Abbas said.

"Now that you'll finish it, Ismail said, "Come to my house at night. And your sister will tell your aunt too. You'll come, yeah?"

"What shall I do with this?" Abbas said.

"Let it go hang around for a while and come yourself." Ismail said.

"No, I can't let it go," Abbas said, "The entire Bayal hates this poor wretch. They may do some harm to him."

"If so, let it loose in the yard and lock the door and come." Ismail said.

Abbas who was cleaning the Khatoonabadian's ears said: "Good idea, sure, I'll do so."

The Redhead who had newly arrived came and sat down beside Abbas and started washing the dog's other ear. And the Khatoonabadian stuck its tongue out and started licking Ismail's hand.

## 12

Early in the night, Abbas went to Ismail's house. His sister had raised smoke behind the ruined wall and was cooking porridge; as soon as she saw that Abbas has appeared she ran forward. She had a large wooden spoon with crushed grains of wheat in her hand.

"I want to tell you something Abbas." Abbas's sister said.

"Tell me sister, tell me." Abbas said.

"I tell you that, accept whatever the Bayalers tell you." Abbas's sister said.

"What do the Bayalers want to tell me?" Abbas said.

"I don't know." Abbas's sister said.

"Hasn't Ismail told you anything?" Abbas said.

"All of them have come and are waiting for you." Abbas's sister said.

Abbas opened the wooden hatch on the wall. He first took his feet and then his trunk and at last his head in. Ismail and Mashdi Baba and Mashdi Jabbar and Abdullah were sitting around a little lamp which was burning in the middle of the room.

"You're so late Mashdi Abbas?" Ismail said.

"Yeah, you're so late." Mashdi Baba said.

"Sure you've been busy and had a lot of work to do." Mashdi Jabbar said.

"I was going to come after it got dark, didn't you tell me to come at night?" Abbas said to Ismail.

"Yeah, you're talking sense, come on now, sit down." Ismail said.

Abbas went and sat between Abdullah and Mashdi Baba, exactly facing the lamp which had a turbid light.

"How are you doing, what news?" Abdullah said.

"Where are the Headman and Islam?" Abbas said.

"They had an emergency and they didn't come." Mashdi Baba said.

"All right," Abbas said, "Did you want just me?" Abbas said.

"Yeah, we want to talk to you." Mashdi Baba said.

"What talk?" Abbas said.

"Yeah," Mashdi Jabbar said, "We want to settle your life."

"What do you mean you want to do?" Abbas said.

"First let's have something to eat and then." Mashdi Baba said.

"By the way, isn't the porridge ready Mashdi Ismail?" Mashdi Jabbar said.

When Ismail rose to go out, Abbas's aunt and his sister came in with the table-cloth and the pot of porridge and sat down beside the men. The Redhead's voice, who was singing, could be heard from the half-open hatch. He was not singing, he was calling a stranger.

## 13

Islam was sitting on the edge of the pool and looking at the shadow of the willow by the black stone for washing the dead in the water when Mashdi Safar's son appeared. Mashdi Safar's son who was walking by the rim of the walls went toward the Headman's house, looked around him and jumped to the other side of the wall.

Bayal was quiet and dark. Mashdi Baba and Abdullah's voices could be heard from Ismail's house. Islam took his cap off and bent and looked at his own dark shadow in the water.

Mashdi Safar's son climbed the wall with the pickaxe in his hand and jumped into the darkness, and the darkness swallowed Mashdi Safar's son.

## 14

The women went out when they had the table cleared. "Mashdi Abbas, we're here to gather our wits and settle your life." Mashdi Baba said to Abbas.

"Yeah," Mashdi Jabbar said, "Since the very day that your sister has come to Ismail's house, you've become sort of different."

"And thank God there was auntie and she attended to you." Abdullah said.

"And it was also because of pains of loneliness that you went and brought an unfortunate, ill-starred, Khatoonabadian dog to Bayal." Mashdi Baba said.

"Besides, if it was a real dog we had no objection." Abdullah said.

"Bayal's Papakh is too better than this Khatoonabadian of yours." Mashdi Jabbar said.

"Sure it is, it has never been a burden on the shoulders of neither acquaintance, nor stranger." Abdullah said.

"Yeah Mashdi Abbas," Mashdi Baba said, "We've come here and have said and heard. We want to get a wife for you."

"And we won't wait for the winter to come." Mashdi Jabbar said, "We'll raise arms today or tomorrow."

"Yeah Mashdi Abbas," Ismail said, "Think about it right now and give all of us the honest answer."

Abbas dropped his head down and sank in thought. Mashdi Baba and Mashdi Jabbar lighted their pipes, and while smiling, watched Abbas.

## 15

Mashdi Safar's son stopped when he was near Abbas's house. The aunt looked from the side of the mat curtain and saw him and she came out with a bowl of porridge. The two of them passed and went to the yard together, to the Khatoonabadian which was standing up, waiting and shaking its tail.

The aunt went forward and put the bowl of porridge on earth. The Khatoonabadian smelled the bowl without appetite and looked at the aunt and Mashdi Safar's son and gazed at the pickaxe that was in Mashdi Safar's son's hand. Mashdi Safar's son took the pickaxe behind his back and hid it.

The aunt went forward and said: "Shoo! Shoo! Eat, eat!"

The Khatoonabadian bent down and started licking the porridge.

"You come over here." Mashdi Safar's son said.

The aunt went and stood behind Mashdi Safar's son's back.

"Auntie, you go out and let me see what I can do." Mashdi Safar's son said.

The aunt went out and crouched on the heap of dust at the other side of the wall and gazed at the Khatoonabadian which had bent down and was licking the porridge with a lack of appetite.

Mashdi Safar's son took another step forward and stopped. He raised the pickaxe with both hands and brought it down like a thunder-bolt and knocked it on the Khatoonabadian's waist. First a noise rose. As if a tree had fallen. Then a helpless howl that suddenly exploded and changed into a horrible, strange roar which all of the Bayalers heard.

The aunt, shocked and dazzled, collapsed by the foot of the wall. Mashdi Safar's son raised and brought down the pickaxe again and quieted the roar.

Islam, who was sitting on the edge of the pool, jumped up in shock and listened to the echo of the Khatoonabadian's groan. The Bayalers rushed out. Mashdi Safar's son, with the pickaxe in his hand, threw himself into the darkness and was lost.

## 16

When Abbas entered the yard, he saw that the Khatoonabadian was dropped there quietly and it did not move. The aunt lighted a lamp and brought it. Abbas bent down and looked. Clotted blood had surrounded the Khatoonabadian and the carcass's head had fallen into the bowl of porridge and the body had folded from the waist. Like a tree broken by the wind. The Bayalers came and gathered upon the walls. Mashdi Jabbar and Mashdi Baba and Abdullah and the Redhead on one side and the Headman and Islam on the other side and the rest from upon the opposite wall gazed at the aunt who was sitting by the carcass and was crying bitterly and at Abbas who, with locked teeth and swollen eyes, was looking at their faces one by one.

"Who has done this?" the Headman said in a loud voice.

Nobody answered.

"Answer, one of you," the Headman said again, "Who has crushed this poor wretch's waist? Who has beheaded it?"

Islam coughed and said nothing. Abbas, who was silently standing over the carcass's head, suddenly cried: "I know who's done this. I know who's crushed this poor wretch's waist, who's thrown his head into the bowl, I'll revenge it, his waist, I'll crush it not once but a hundred times, I won't cut off his head, I'll smash it."

He came out of the yard and went to the Headman's house like a thunder-bolt. He jumped over the wall and appeared some moments later with the pickaxe in his hand and he came to the side of the pool and looked at Mashdi Safar's house that was quiet and dark and he ran to the head of the first alley.

The Redhead appeared and said: "Mashdi Abbas, Mashdi Abbas, he ran away and went toward Hazavan, he went toward Hazavan."

Abbas, with foaming mouth, ran out from the alley while howling, and took the rim of the valley and went toward Hazavan.

## 17

The Headman grabbed the Redhead by the head and shouted: "Why did you tell him? Now he'll find and kill him."

Mashdi Baba and Abdullah took the Redhead out of the Headman's grip. Mashdi Jabbar said: "He's not gone, he's not gone to Hazavan, he's in Bayal, in their own house."

When the Headman turned, he saw that Islam was dragging the carcass toward Landlord's garden and the aunt was following him with the lantern, and Mashdi Jabbar was holding the Khatoonabadian's head, which he was taking by the ear, in a distance from himself so that the blood wouldn't drip on his clothes.

# Sixth Story

## 1

It was early in the evening when Mashdi Jabbar entered Bayal; the Bayalers were sitting around at the little square behind Mashdi Safar's house and were chatting.

As soon as the Headman saw Mashdi Jabbar he said: "Hallo Mashdi Jabbar, welcome back, what news from the city?"

"There was no news in the city, no news at all." Mashdi Jabbar said.

"Did you come on foot?" Mashdi Baba said.

Mashdi Jabbar sat down beside Islam and while taking off his shoes and panting with thirst said: "From the roadside to here, yeah."

"When did you reach the roadside?" Islam said.

"It was just a little past noon." Mashdi Jabbar said.

"Why are you so late then?" the Headman said, "Have you been on the way all this time?"

"Yeah," Mashdi Jabbar said, "I encountered a strange thing in the middle of the way and had to wait."

"A strange thing?" Mashdi Safar's son said, "What was it?"

"By God, I couldn't find anything, though I thought a lot." Mashdi Jabbar said.

"You didn't find out? How didn't you find out?" The Headman said.

The men came closer and circled around Mashdi Jabbar, Mashdi Jabbar took Islam's pipe and gave several puffs and said: "It was a big thing, I couldn't find out what it was."

"What did it look like?" Mashdi Baba said.

"Something big. Like a cow. I couldn't move it, though I did my best."

"What did it look like? Did it have head and ears? Didn't it? What did it look like?" Abdullah said.

Mashdi Jabbar thought and said: "I couldn't find out... eyes and ears... it had none."

"What about limbs?" the Headman said.

"Limbs?" Mashdi Jabbar said, "No, it had no limbs either, because it was too heavy."

"What did it look like?" Islam said.

Mashdi Jabbar thought again and said: "How can I say? But it wasn't like a cart."

"But at first you said it was like a cow." Mashdi Baba said.

"Yeah," Mashdi Jabbar said, "It was as big as a cow, just somehow a little bit more well-set than a cow."

"But you said it had no limbs." The Headman said.

"Yeah, and I say it again." Mashdi Jabbar said, "It had no limbs or eyes or ears or the like of them."

"Whom did it look like?" Ismail said.

Mashdi Jabbar thought and then examined every man and house one by one. He coughed several times and said: "It looked like nobody. It was a strange thing. Like a ... by God, I don't know what to say!"

"How did it walk?" Abdullah said.

"As for walking, it didn't," Mashdi Jabbar said, "There was no head or neck or the like of them about. It was a strange thing like a small house. Like Baba Ali's house with large buttons around it."

"What was it made of?" Islam said.

"I don't know if it was tin or iron or something else." Mashdi Jabbar said.

"It wasn't a wrecked car, was it?" Islam said.

"Oh no," Mashdi Jabbar said, "It had no wheels or the like of them. And it was too heavy."

"Where did you see it?" the Headman asked.

"Just several steps over-by "Shoor", on the way to Pooruss." Mashdi Jabbar said.

"Aha," Islam said, "I'm getting it now."

All of the men looked at Islam. The Headman said: "What are you getting Mashdi Islam?"

"If there's anything, there's those Poorussians' hand in it," Islam said, "Now they've stolen it from somewhere and have thrown it in the middle of the way."

"He's right, it's the Poorussian's work." Mashdi Jabbar said.

All of the men sank in thought.

"Ok, what do you say we shall do?" Mashdi Baba said.

"It's clear," Mashdi Safar's son said, "We'll go and see what it is, is it of use or not!"

Islam looked at the sky and around the pool and said: "It's getting dark, soon it'll be night."

"Don't worry about the night son." Mashdi Baba said.

"What do you say Mashdi Islam?" the Headman said.

"Let's go," Islam said, "Let's go and see what it is."

"Can you bring us a couple of lanterns Mashdi Jafar?" the headman said to Mashdi Safar's son.

Mashdi Safar's son rose and said: "Why not."

And he went hurriedly. "Yeah," Islam said, "Let's go see what it is. If it was of any use, so we'll bring it to Bayal. If it wasn't, so we'll leave it to God's care."

"By what will you go Mashdi Islam?" Mashdi Baba said.

"It's clear," Islam said, "We'll put the horse before the cart and go by the cart."

"All right," the Headman said, "Let's move before it's late."

The men rose. It was near sunset. The moon, pale and swollen, was rising from the direction of Pooruss.

## 2

After having dinner, they came and gathered by the edge of the pool. Islam put the horse before the cart and took the cart under the willow, beside the black stone for washing the dead. Ismail and Mashdi Safar's son came to the men with two lanterns, they put the lanterns on the cart and waited.

"Why have you lighted the lanterns?" the Headman said.

"You yourself said so Headman." Mashdi Jabbar said.

"The sky is light, can't you see the moon?" the Headman said.

He pointed at the pool. The men turned and watched the moon in the pool.

"You yourself told me to bring lanterns, didn't you?" Mashdi Safar's son said.

"Lanterns are necessary." Mashdi Jabbar said, "If there's no lantern we can't find out what it is."

Islam's black goat groaned from inside the store. The sound of the crickets was heard from the Landlord's garden.

"The lanterns will run out of oil till we reach Shoor," the Headman said, "We will be on the way for an hour and a bit more."

"Put them out," Mashdi Baba said to Mashdi Safar's son, "We'll light them when we reached Shoor."

Mashdi Jabbar turned the wicks down and blew. The lanterns went out. Islam, who was sitting on a tree trunk, loudly asked: "Ok, who's coming?"

"He's right, anyway, everyone cannot come." The Headman said.

"I say the young ones must go," Mashdi Baba said, "Firstly, they're stronger. Secondly, if they face any Poorussians, they can run away immediately and if they got caught, they can give them a good lesson."

"This 'young ones' means who?" the Headman said.

"I and you are now too old to do such things Headman." Mashdi Baba said, "The young ones means Mashdi Ismail, Mashdi Jabbar, Mashdi Jafar and Abdullah. And Mashdi Islam must go too."

"You want to say that you're not coming?" Islam said.

"Because, I...," Mashdi Baba said.

"For shame Mashdi Baba, get up and get on the cart." Islam said.

Mashdi Baba rose. They went to the cart. Bayal was quiet and dark, only the howling of several dogs could be heard from afar. Mashdi Safar who had raised his head out of the roof-hole was watching the shadows of the men who were getting on the cart, and the pale moon which was being distorted and enlarging and shrinking in the pool.

### 3

When the men were gone, Granny Khanoom and Granny Fatimah appeared who passed the first alley and came out of Bayal and went toward the *Nabi Agha* hill.

It was Thursday night. The old women were going to bring dust from Nabi Agha for healing the sick.

### 4

The desert was lighted. The horse was galloping forward hastily and carrying the men who were sitting squatted on the cart. Islam was whirling the whip around his head in the moonlight and shouting loudly: "Ho, ho, ho!"

Hearing the howl of the whip the horse would gallop faster. Ismail was sitting side by side with Islam and singing. The men were leaning against each other. Mashdi Jabbar had the put-out lanterns in his arms. The Headman had taken Mashdi Safar's son's pipe and he regularly emptied and filled it. They descended the slopes in a way as if they were falling into a well. The horse and its shadow were larger than usual. Islam was watching the desert in wonder. All of them were happy. Except Mashdi Baba who had put his head on his knee indignantly and was dozing off or grumbling in whispers.

## 5

Before Reaching Shoor, Islam pulled the horse's harness. The cart stopped. "Are we there?" the Headman said.

"Nearly," Islam said, "Ok, where did you see it Mashdi Jabbar?"

"Farther than here. On the narrow path which goes toward Pooruss." Mashdi Jabbar said.

"So I must go farther?" Islam said.

"No Mashdi Islam," Mashdi Baba said, "Don't go toward Pooruss. For God's sake don't get us into trouble."

The men laughed. Islam raised the whip. The cart started moving again. When they reached Shoor, they fell into silence and darkness. The sound f the wheels and the horse's steps could not be heard anymore. And there was no other noise either. Mashdi Jabbar was pressing the put-out lanterns in his arms.

Mashdi Baba asked Abdullah softly: "Where are they going to go?"

Islam laughed and Mashdi Safar's son said: "We're going to the heart of Pooruss."

"Don't joke," Mashdi Baba said, "Mashdi Islam will never do such a thing."

"Don't worry Mashdi Baba," Islam said, "Even if we went to Pooruss the Poorussians would never hurt *you*."

"Even so, it's still better not to go. Am I right Headman?" Mashdi Baba said.

Islam laughed. When the cart was on the narrow path to Pooruss, three Poorussians appeared on horses and Passed before the cart and took the by-way like thunder-bolts. Mashdi Baba hid behind the others. Islam stopped the cart. The Bayalers quietly watched the three Poorussians who were rushing toward Mishoo.

"Didn't I tell you Islam? Didn't I?" Mashdi Baba said.

"But they didn't do anything to us." The Headman said.

Islam laughed. Mashdi Safar's son said: "Let's go Mashdi Islam!"

The cart started moving and Islam said: "Let us know when we're there Mashdi Jabbar."

"Looks like it was just around here." Mashdi Jabbar said.

Islam stopped the cart. The Bayalers looked around them.

"Where is it?" the Headman said.

"Let's get off." Mashdi Jabbar said, "Let's get off."

All of the men got off. Mashdi Safar's son lighted one of the lanterns and handed it to Mashdi Jabbar and took the put-out lantern himself; all of them started walking shoulder to shoulder with each other.

"Where are we going?" Ismail said, "If we're going to go farther, it's better to get on the cart again."

Mashdi Jabbar stopped and looked around him in surprise and said: "It was around here."

"Haven't we mistaken the way?" Mashdi Safar's son said.

"No we haven't," Mashdi Jabbar said, "It was just around here."

He held the lantern up and bent down and started watching the earth. Mashdi Safar's son burst into laughter and Islam also laughed. "What are you looking for Mashdi Jabbar?" the

Headman said, "You were saying that it was very big and couldn't be moved?"

All of the men laughed. Mashdi Jabbar didn't answer. He was looking for some obscure thing on the earth.

## 6

Granny Khanoom and Granny Fatimah were sitting on the platform on the threshold of Nabi Agha; they were waiting for the tumult of the come-and-goes of the tomb to come to an end, so that they could go in. Bayal was below their feet, Landlord's garden before them, and the large pool which from among the houses and under the pale moonlight, was looking at the sky like a corpse's eye.

When the tumult decreased, Granny Khanoom rose and opened the door of the tomb and went into the darkness. She lighted a candle carefully. When the mice saw the candlelight they rushed toward the shrine and went in by the holes in the chest. Granny Fatimah who was standing before the door said in a soft voice: "O Allah, O Your Holiness, O Ali, O Muhammad, O Hassan, O Hossein, Hail thee Your Holiness, O Ali, O Muhammad, O Hassan, O Hossein, We've come to take dust for healing, O Your Holiness, O Imam, O Ali, O Allah, heal the sick of Bayal! Heal them yourself!"

## 7

Mashdi Jabbar was bent down and walking under the light of the lantern, looking around, and the Bayalers were slowly walking after him.

"What if something's wrong with Mashdi Jabbar?" Ismail said.

"Nothing's wrong with him, he's playing the fool!" Mashdi Safar's son said.

"Mashdi Jabbar, Mashdi Jabbar!" Islam said, "What's wrong with you? Why do you do that?"

Mashdi Jabbar sat down and suddenly cried: "Here it is, I've found it, I've found it!"

The men circled around Mashdi Jabbar and bent down. Mashdi Jabbar pointed at the ground and said: "It's been right here, they've taken it away. Do you see Mashdi Islam? Do you see Mashdi Baba?"

"He's right," Islam said, "Something has been here which has left a trace on the earth."

"What's happened?" the Headman said, "How have they taken it away? Who's taken it away?"

"For sure the Poorussians have taken it," Mashdi Safar's son said, "You didn't move soon enough, and they've come and taken it."

Mashdi Jabbar, bent down, walked and reached the edge of the valley and raised the lantern and looked unto the valley and cried: "Hey Mashdi Islam, hey Headman, it's here, in the valley."

The Bayalers hurried to the edge of the valley and bent down. On the slope in the valley, a big metal chest was fallen on one side and was shining under the moonlight.

"Is that it Mashdi Jabbar?" Islam said.

"Yeah, that's it! That's it!" Mashdi Jabbar said.

First Mashdi Jabbar and then the men descended the slope in the valley; Mashdi Jabbar walked around the chest and said: "Yeah, that's it." Mashdi Safar's son sat on the earth and took the put-out lantern from Islam and lighted it and went forward. He walked around the chest and sat down beside the others and put the lantern before his own face.

"Who's thrown it here?" Islam said.

"It wasn't here first when I saw it, it was up there." Mashdi Jabbar said.

"For sure it's the Poorussians." The Headman said.

"It's good we found it." Islam said.

Mashdi Baba took out his pipe and tobacco bag and said: "What do you think it can be Mashdi Jabbar?"

"It's a chest, a tin chest." Abdullah said.

"It's clear that it's a chest, but what's in it?" Mashdi Baba said.

Abdullah rose and walked around the chest and said: "It's got no door, when it's got no door, you can't find out what's in it."

"When it's got no door, it's got no inside either to be full or empty." Ismail said.

"Maybe it's a car which has capsized and become like that." Abdullah said.

"Oh no," Islam said, "It's not a car, if it was a car it had wheels."

"What about the bath thing?" the Headman said.

"What bath thing?" Islam said in surprise.

"One of those things that we saw in the city, on Agha Enayat's roof?" the Headman said.

"No," Islam said, "The inside of that was empty and they had poured water in it. And it wasn't like this."

"It's nothing," Mashdi Safar's son said, "It's wholly iron."

"Who's seen iron like this?" the Headman said.

"And besides, of what use can it be? What's the use for this?" Mashdi Baba said.

"You can make boilers out of it," Mashdi Safar's son said, "You can make pots out of it. And you can make lots of other things."

Islam, while looking at the chest in a kind of ecstasy, said: "No, it's not iron. It's not a simple thing. Do you see its walls? Do you see its lattices? Do you see its buttons?"

"Mashdi Islam is right," the Headman said, "It must be quiet a thing for itself. And a very important thing it must be too."

"Whatever it is, I don't think it's a useful thing." Mashdi Safar's son said.

"If it was useful, the Poorussians wouldn't throw it away." Abdullah said.

"Maybe they weren't strong enough to take it with them." Islam said.

"For God's sake Mashdi Islam," the Headman said, "Get up and see what it is."

Islam rose and went toward the chest. He touched and inspected. He sat down beside the chest, dallied with its buttons. The moon was shining on the chest and particles of light were scattered in every direction. "What is it?", Islam said to himself, "What can it be?"

He took his head forward and stuck his face on the chest and put his ear on it and listened. Suddenly, he rose hastily. The men looked at him.

"Get up, come and listen!" Islam said, "Headman! Come on Mashdi Baba! Come on Ismail!"

The men rose and went forward and put their ears on the trunk of the chest.

"Do you hear?" Islam said.

"Yeah, yeah." The Headman said.

"But I can't hear anything." Mashdi Safar's son said.

"Listen carefully." Islam said.

He sat down beside the others himself and put his ear on the wall of the chest and again said: "Do you hear?"

"I can hear something." Mashdi Baba said.

"He's right, there's something." Ismail said.

"But I can't hear anything." Mashdi Safar's son said.

"Are you listening Headman?" Islam said.

"It's as if the wind is blowing inside it." The Headman said.

"No sir, it's water." Mashdi Baba said.

"Maybe they've put a bunch of bees and flies in it?" Ismail said.

"I hear nothing" Mashdi Safar's son said.

Islam raised his head and said: "No, it's no other sound. They're crying inside it. It's the sound of crying and wailing."

The men stuck their ears to the trunk of the chest and rose in horror.

"Yeah," the Headman said, "By God's rule it's the sound of crying."

"You mean there's someone inside it who's crying and wailing?" Mashdi Baba said.

"Nobody's crying and wailing inside it," Islam said, "It's a shrine. The zarih of a shrine. Don't you see how it looks like? You heard the sound of the crying, didn't you?"

"As for me, I didn't hear." Mashdi Safar's son said.

The men walked backwards and sat down on the earth.

"What shall we do now Mashdi Islam?" the Headman said.

"We'll take it to Bayal. We'll take it to Bayal." Islam said.

"Take it to Bayal to do what with?" Mashdi Baba said, "Take and throw it beside the others in the banner-house?"

"We'll take it now and then I'll tell you what to do." Islam said.

The neighing of Islam's horse was heard from the road. Mashdi Safar's son hurriedly went upward; a Poorussian with dagger in his hand was hanging around the cart and watching them. As soon as Mashdi Safar's son appeared, he ran away like the wind and disappeared in the darkness of the edge of the valley.

## 8

When they were near Bayal, it was past midnight. Granny Fatimah and Granny Khanoom came with two lighted lanterns and sat by Landlord's garden. It was cold and the moon had moved westward. Islam had taken the horse's harness and was pulling it; the men were all walking on foot, panting and were pushing the cart forward. The chest was on the cart. Granny Khanoom and Granny Fatimah who were sitting outside the village rose and approached. Islam stopped the cart and the men stopped and came forward panting.

"What's this Mashdi Islam?" Granny Khanoom said.

"This... this is a zarih Mashdi Khanoom." Islam said.

"What? A zarih?" Granny Fatimah said.

"Yeah," Islam said, "It's a zarih, it's an Agha, it's a shrine." Granny Khanoom went closer hurriedly and held the lantern up and looked the chest in wonder and beat her breast and said: "O *Stranger among strangers*, O Imam of our times."

Granny Fatimah said: "Hail to thee O Muhammad O Your Holiness O Fatimah O Ali."

"Hail to thee o the Blood of God." Islam said.

"Hail to thee o *Imam of Strangers*." The Headman said.

The men came closer and circled around the cart. The old women sat down opposite to the cart. Islam climbed the cart and kissed the chest and cried. The men and the women cried.

Islam chanted dirges loudly. The men rose and beat their breasts and chanted dirges. Mashdi Safar woke up and put his head out of the roof-hole and looked. He saw that the Bayalers have come out of the houses and are going out of the village.

## 9

In the morning they brought the cart to the front of Islam's house. The old women circled and sat around the cart. The Headman and Islam and Mashdi Jabbar went to find a place for the chest.

"I say the back of Mashdi Safar's house is better than anywhere else." Mashdi Jabbar said.

"It's not better at all," Islam said, "It needs an eye-catching place so that it can be seen even from outside the village."

"He's right," the Headman said, "The little square is low, and besides, no one passes by the little square."

"So where shall we put it?" Mashdi Jabbar said.

"The height beside the banner-house is better than anywhere else." Islam said.

"Bravo Mashdi Islam, well said!" the Headman said.

"All right, let's take it to the side of the banner-house." Mashdi Jabbar said.

They returned and went to the front of Islam's house again and took the cart to the head of the alley and passed behind the Headman's house and reached beside the banner-house.

"What are you doing?" Mashdi Baba said, "Are you going to take it inside the banner-house?"

"No, we're taking it to the top of that height." Islam said, "We'll build walls all around it and we'll cover its roof in autumn."

"Good idea Mashdi Islam. A very good idea." The Headman said.

"No one shall go to the desert today till we finish it." Islam said.

"Yeah, no one shall go. And today is Friday too." The Headman said.

Islam took his cap off and put it on the cart and turned to the Redhead and said: "Run and bring some shovels and pick-axes."

The Headman drew a line around the height with a taw and said: "We'll build four walls, won't we Mashdi Islam?"

"Yeah, we'll build four walls." Islam said.

"Is this piece of land enough?" the Headman said.

"Sure it's enough." Islam said.

"In how many days would it finish?" Mashdi Baba said.

"We'll finish it this very day." Islam said.

"Who's going to bring water?" Mashdi Baba said.

"Everyone," the Headman said, "This work's got a very great reward. Everyone will be rewarded for it by Imam Hossein."

"I'll bring water, I'll make clay and I'll do anything else that you say." Ismail said.

"I too will bring water." Abdullah said.

"A real tomb will be built," Granny Fatimah said, "We'll raise the banners, we'll bring the chandeliers and the palms too. We'll arrange them around the zarih."

"O Imam Hossein, I ask for your mercy." Granny Khanoom said.

"We'll put the zarih in the center and then we'll raise the walls." Islam said.

The men went to the cart. The Redhead appeared with shovels and pick-axes. The old women went toward the banner-house. Mashdi Zeinal came with the crutches and sat in front of the door of the banner-house. The sunshine spread, and no one went to the desert from Bayal.

## 10

It was not long past the noon when they built four short clay walls on the hill. The men came to the side of the pool. They washed their hands and feet and stretched in a line in the shadow. The women had put a large boiler on fire beside the black stone for washing the dead and the oblatory pottage was boiling, burbling and steaming.

"You see how soon it finished?" the Headman said.

"By God, it was a miracle." Mashdi Baba said.

"The Aghas helped us." Islam said.

"You can see God's hand in this one. The saints and the prophets themselves helped." Granny Khanoom said.

"It's so good." Granny Fatimah said, "We'll bring here the sick who couldn't be taken to the token."

"And you know that it needs a janitor too." The Headman said.

Baba Ali who had put his head out of the hatch of the enclosure said: "Mashdi Zeinal's very good for this job."

The men turned and looked at Mashdi Zeinal.

"It would be too better if we had a *Seyed*.[8]" Islam said.

"How about going and bringing someone from Seyedabad?" Mashdi Safar's son said.

"My mother was a *Seyed*, Granny Khanoom knows that." Mashdi Zeinal said.

"Yeah, the God-forgiven *Seyed* Fatimah," Granny Khanoom said, "Who used to go begging in the neighborhood."

"Thank God that this is also settled." The Headman said.

"I'm dying out of hunger." Mashdi Safar's son said.

The women brought the pots. Granny Fatimah prayed. The women arranged the pots on the earth. Granny Khanoom rolled her sleeves up and went to the pot of pottage. And Granny Fatimah was dividing pieces of bread among the men.

---

[8] Descendant of the prophet.

## 11

In the evening Granny Khanoom and Granny Fatimah went to the banner-house. They first brought the large icon out and then the banners and then the palms and chandeliers. They took the icon and leant it against the wall opposite to the door of the zarih. They settled four banners on the four corners of the enclosure. They put the palms in the chandeliers and arranged the chandeliers on the chest and lighted the candles.

Islam wrapped a green turban around Mashdi Zeinal's head. Mashdi Zeinal, with the crutches, came and sat on the threshold and started reciting Quran.

The old women went to the sick of the Bayal. They raised Mashdi Akbar's infirm son and Abdullah's sister on their hands and brought them to the shrine. Granny Khanoom tied chains around the necks of the sick and knitted the chains to the big buttons of the chest and said: "Cry and take your cure from Agha."

The sick stretched on the dust and started wailing. Granny Fatimah who had taken ablution came and stood before the threshold and loudly said: "O Allah, O your Holiness, O Ali, o Muhammad, O Hassan, O Hossein, Hail to thee O Allah, O your Holiness, O Ali, O Muhammad, O Hassan, O Hossein. We've come and we want cure. O your Holiness O Imam O Prophet O Ali O Allah, cure the sick of Bayal. Cure them yourself."

The Bayalers who were standing behind Granny Fatimah raised their hands and said in a chorus: "Amen."

## 12

Two big trucks were searching the entire neighborhood. First they went to Pooruss; they looked in all of the houses and wells.

Then they went to Seyedabad, Khatoonabad, Malekzadeh, Yengijeh, Hassanabad, Mishoo; they searched all of the houses. But they didn't go to Bayal. Bayal was small, it was very small.

They were returning from Hazavan when they reached the slope of Shoor, the first truck stopped. The second one also stopped. An American sergeant got off the truck and looked at Bayal with binoculars and gave a sign to go there. The sergeant who was standing behind the American said: "There's nothing there."

The American gave a sign, the trucks started moving toward Bayal.

It was almost evening. The men were sitting at the back of Mashdi Safar's house and were chatting. When they heard the noise of the trucks, they rose and ran toward the desert. The trucks stopped. First the American and then the soldiers got off and rushed into the village. They looked at the clay houses and the short roofs. Nothing could be seen. The American went toward the banner-house. Mashdi Zeinal who was sitting in the threshold of the zarih started reciting Quran. The American went forward and when he looked inside the tomb, started shouting. The soldiers ran forward and looked. The American gave a sign. One of the soldiers opened a suitcase which he had in his hand. The American entered. He untied the chains from around Mashdi Akbar's son and Abdullah's sister's neck. The old women came in and took the sick ones out. The American looked around him in surprise and then hit the chandeliers and the palms and threw all of them down. The soldier brought out two wires from the suitcase and tied them to two buttons of the chest and took the wires and knitted them to another metal chest which had several big lights and then went behind the chest. And the Bayalers ascended and circled all around and stared at the inside of the enclosure. The American put his foot on a small pedal and pushed. The chest started making noises and roared. The lights were switched on and flamed. The Bayalers were frightened and walked backwards.

The American roared. The soldiers rushed and ruined the walls. One of the trucks came to the side of the height and the soldiers lifted the chest and put it in the truck. Then they returned and surrounded the Bayalers.

A short sergeant said: "Where have you taken it from?"

"We've found it on the way." The Headman said.

"On which way?" the Sergeant said.

"It was fallen on the way to Pooruss." The Headman said.

"Which one of you brought it?" the sergeant said.

"All of us." Islam said.

The sergeant gave a sign to the soldiers and said: "Mount them all."

Mashdi Safar's son who was standing farther shouted: "Mashdi Jabbar has brought it, not all of us. Mashdi Jabbar found it and he came and told us. It's all Mashdi Jabbar's fault."

"Which one of you is Mashdi Jabbar?" the sergeant said.

And he looked at the men. "There he is." Mashdi Safar's son said.

And he pointed at Mashdi Jabbar who was standing beside Mashdi Baba and Islam. The soldiers went and took Mashdi Jabbar toward the truck. The American got on. They mounted Mashdi Jabbar too. The soldiers cursed and got on. The Bayalers were frightened and they walked backwards and hid behind the walls. When the trucks started moving the Redhead said to Abdullah: "Good for Mashdi Jabbar who having not still arrived from the city returned to the city again."

## 13

When the trucks were away Granny Fatimah and Granny Khanoom went and collected the banners and the palms and chandeliers and took them to the banner-house.

Islam and the Headman pushed the dust aside with shovels and brought the icon out. When the night came the men came and gathered beside the pool. And the women went and sat behind the wall. Islam climbed the black stone for washing the dead and chanted dirges.

The Bayalers cried bitterly, for Agha and for the lost zarih.

# Seventh Story

## 1

Islam and Mashdi Baba and Mashdi Safar's son brought the Redhead beside the pool and seated him under the willow, beside the black stone for washing the dead. Islam had a bag of stale bread under his arm from which he was taking out pieces and putting them in the Redhead's mouth. And the red haired one chewed quickly and swallowed greedily. Ismail and Abdullah and the Headman also came and sat down.

"Say, what shall we do to him?" Mashdi Baba said.

"As for me, I'm at my wit's end." The Headman said, "We had seen everything but this one, one is struck dumb why he wouldn't get full at all."

"How's that, he eats that much and doesn't burst?" Mashdi Safar's son said.

Abdullah coughed loudly and said: "How his looks have changed, do you see his eyes? Do you see his mouth?"

Ismail brought two potatoes out of his pocket and put them in the Redhead's mouth and said: "His limbs have sort of changed too."

Mashdi Safar's son took the Redhead's hand and looked at his palm and said: "It has grown wool and become broad, just like a bear's claw."

"The way he eats, nothing can be found in Bayal in a month." Islam said.

The Redhead, whose mouth was empty, roared: "I'm hungry, I'm hungry."

"I wish you would burst! How much do you eat?" Mashdi Baba said.

Islam put several pieces of bread in the Redhead's mouth. The Redhead swallowed the bread wholly and again roared: "I'm hungry."

Ismail put two other potatoes in the Redhead's mouth and said: "Last night he's gone to Granny Fatimah's house and has eaten all the cabbages and potatoes and onions that's been there."

"And three nights ago he's come and swallowed all of my father's wheat." Mashdi Safar's son said.

"He had come to our house too, when I threw him down from on the wall with a club." Abdullah said.

Ismail put another potato in the Redhead's mouth and said: "My wife has taken and hidden everything we had out of fear."

The Redhead swallowed the potato and cried: "I'm hungry, I'm hungry."

"By God Islam, don't give him anything to eat and let's see what he would do?" the Headman said.

Islam and the others ceased and didn't give him anything.

The Redhead shouted louder: "I'm hungry, I'm hungry, I'm hungry!"

"Give him something man, my eardrum is being torn off." Mashdi Baba said.

Islam put a piece of bread in the Redhead's mouth and said: "All right, All right, don't shout."

"What shall we do to him?" the Headman said.

"As far as I can see, in a month all of us must go begging to be able to fill this creature's stomach." Islam said.

"You mean all of us must go begging and give it to him to eat?" Mashdi Baba said.

"Don't you see to what condition he's come?" Islam said.

Ismail put another potato in the Redhead's mouth and said: "If so, it must be thought about from right now. As for me, I don't feel like begging and knocking on this and that door."

"Isn't it better to give him straw and grass to eat instead of bread?" the Headman said.

"These things won't do," Mashdi Safar's son said, "It has only one way. Just one way."

The men looked at each other. "What way?" Abdullah said.

"Making short work of it." Mashdi Safar's son said.

"I'm hungry, I'm hungry." The Redhead cried.

Ismail handed two potatoes to the Redhead and said: "It's a sin son, and a very big sin it is too!"

"I won't let you do that." Islam said.

"So what will you do to him?" Mashdi Safar's son said.

Islam thought and said: "I say, let's take and throw him in some place and lock the door and leave some bread and water for him too."

"He'll starve to death." Ismail said.

"So much the better," Islam said, "So much the better if he starves to death, and if he didn't, we'll cut an amount from his food and water each day so that he may come to his senses."

"Where do you take him?" Abdullah said.

The Headman was happy and said: "Bravo Islam, bravo Mashdi Islam, what a good idea! May God grant you a long life!"

Islam pointed his hand at a corner. The men turned happily and looked at the ruined mill fallen on the way to Jamishan. When they rose the Redhead started shouting and roared: "I'm hungry, I'm hungry!"

## 2

When the door of the mill opened, the mice ran away and hid under an old coffin. Islam entered. Mashdi Baba and Mashdi Safar's son pushed the Redhead. Then all of them entered. The mill had no firm door or windows, its roof had collapsed and sunshine was cast on the walls which still bore the remains of white color from the flour leftovers.

Ismail gave the water jar he had in his hand to Abdullah and brought two potatoes out of his pocket and put them in the Redhead's mouth and said: "Good, this place is very good for him!"

Mashdi Baba put the bag full of carrots by the wall and said: "But it has no roof Mashdi Islam?"

"Ok, let it have no roof, what would happen?" Ismail said.

"He may get ideas and run away." Mashdi Baba said.

"The walls are high, he can't run away." Islam said.

Mashdi Safar's son put the large can of pottage beside the bag of carrots and leant the jar of water against the can of pottage. The Headman examined the broken door and said: "But this door has no firm latch or hasp, what do you want to do about it Mashdi Islam?"

"We'll fix it, never mind." Islam said.

The Headman brought some pieces of bread and a handful of carrots out of the bags and poured them on the coffin before the Redhead. The Redhead started eating and the men watched him and came out. Islam closed the door and said: "We must nail the door, there's no other way!"

"Shall we break the door and get in tomorrow?" Ismail said.

"We'll bring a ladder and put it at this side of the wall and throw anything we like down from up there." Islam said.

"How many days should he stay in there Mashdi Islam?" Ismail said.

Islam thought and said: "It's not clear, God knows. Maybe one day and maybe a hundred days; and maybe he got well and we brought him out sooner."

"You think that he may get well?" the Headman said.

"Maybe he gets well and maybe he doesn't get well." Islam said, "Everything is in God's hand."

"If he doesn't get well we shouldn't let him in the village, he'll spoil everyone's life." Mashdi Safar's son said.

The Redhead, who was sitting on the coffin with full mouth, roared: "I'm hungry, I'm hungry!"

## 3

At the night the mice came out from under the coffin and came close slowly and circled around the Redhead who had finished the large can of pottage and was gnashing at the carrots. As soon as the Redhead saw the mice, he rose with full mouth and started trampling on them. The mice rushed and filled the empty can. The Redhead picked up the bag of carrots and the bag of bread and took them and put them on the coffin and sat on the other corner of the coffin himself. When the moon rose, it lighted the inside of the mill. The Redhead stopped chewing and listened. No sound could be heard except the noise of the mice which had gone into the can and were licking the walls with appetite, and a strange noise, as if, far away, hundreds of pottage pots were boiling and burbling.

## 4

It was past midnight when Islam suddenly woke up. A big, black figure had plunged into the pool and was flouncing. He ran out by the window. The other men also came out. They saw the Redhead who had sunk in the water up to the throat and was chasing the fish under the moonlight.

The Headman looked in surprise. Mashdi Baba brought a lantern and held it up and said: "May God protect us all, what's he gone there for?"

The Headman cried: "Hey kid, what are you doing in there?"

The Redhead was flouncing in the pool and attacking the fish.

"Come out! Come out!" Islam said.

"What have you gone there for?" the Headman said.

"I'm hungry!" the Redhead said.

"You ate all the victuals?" Ismail said.

The Redhead cried: "I'm hungry! I'm hungry!"

"Sure he has finished them all that he's come out." The Headman said.

"How has he come out?" Mashdi Safar's son said.

The Headman put his hands around his mouth and called the Redhead: "Come out kid, come out."

The Redhead whose mouth was filled with water replied: "I'm hungry." And he attacked the fish. "Why does he do that?" Ismail said.

"Can't you see?" Mashdi Baba said, "He's going to catch the fish and swallow them."

"How does he want to swallow them?" Ismail said, "They aren't edible, anyone who eats them is immediately done for."

"So much the better," Mashdi Safar's son said, "Now that it's so, let him eat and be done for!"

The Headman took the lantern from Mashdi Baba's hand and waved it and said: "Come out kid, come out!"

"He won't come out this way," Islam said, "He won't come out unless we show him victuals."

"I'll go and bring something right now." Ismail said.

He went away and came back with two loaves of bread. Islam took the bread and showed it to the Redhead and said: "Hey kid, come on, bread, bread, won't you have bread?"

The Redhead came out of the pool hurriedly and ran toward Islam, and Islam tore off the loaves of bread and crammed them into the Redhead's mouth. "What are you going to do to him now?" the Headman said to Islam.

"We need ropes," Islam said, "Bring a firm rope so that we take and tie him that he can't run away and come out."

"But ropes wouldn't do," Mashdi Safar's son said, "We tie him and he immediately unties it and runs away."

"We'll tie him in a way that he can't untie it." Islam said.

"Shall we take him to the mill again?" the Headman said.

"Yeah," Islam said, "If he stays in the village he'll make scenes and his noise wouldn't let anybody sleep. It's necessary to take victuals for him too."

Ismail brought a rope. The men took the Redhead's limbs and dragged him toward the mill. Mashdi Baba, with lantern in his hand, was walking in the front and lighting the way. Mashdi Safar had put his head out of the roof-hole, and he thought that the Bayalers were heading toward Jamishan.

## 5

First Mashdi Baba, with the lantern in his hand, entered the mill and went forward. The mice ran away and hid under the coffin. Islam and Mashdi Safar's son pushed the Redhead in. All of them entered. The moon was right over their heads and they could see the junk in the mill very clearly.

"So, he has broken the door and come out." Abdullah said.

"It's Islam's fault who hasn't fastened the door properly." Mashdi Safar's son said.

"I thought that if he even ate till tomorrow noon he couldn't finish that much victuals we left for him." Islam said.

Mashdi Safar's son kicked the empty can and said: "Look, he's eaten it wholly and still hasn't burst."

Ismail put the bundle of bread and onions on the coffin and said: "He'll eat and finish these in half an hour and he'll be out again."

"As a rule of thumb, nothing can be found in Bayal in two days!" Mashdi Safar's son said.

"I'm afraid he would break into the stacks and eat and finish the whole wheat." The Headman said.

"Better go and bring some straw and alfalfa for him." Mashdi Safar's son said.

"It can't be helped." Islam said, "Now, who knows how to knit this rope firmly?"

"I know." Mashdi Safar's son said.

"In a way that he can't untie it." Islam said.

"I'll knit it in a way that he wouldn't be able to open it in two years." Mashdi Safar's son said.

"And Abdullah and I will go and bring alfalfa." Ismail said.

And they went away. The men sat around the Redhead. The Redhead was busy, swallowing the pieces of bread quickly when Islam took his right leg and raised it. Mashdi Safar's son looped the rope twice and cast them around the Redhead's ankles like two anklets. Mashdi Baba brought the lantern closer. Mashdi Safar's son knitted a big, queer knot on the rope which made Islam and the Headman laugh. Mashdi Safar's son rose and tied the other end of the rope to a large millstone which was dropped in the corner of the enclosure. They waited and watched the Redhead. Ismail and Abdullah appeared with two armfuls of alfalfa. They poured the alfalfa on the coffin. Mashdi Baba took the lantern, all of them came out. The moonlight had paled and the darkness of the night had flown and a milky strip was rising from the East.

## 6

In the evening, when they returned from the desert, they found the Redhead in front of Baba Ali's house, whom women and children had surrounded, and had poured potatoes and carrots and turnips and alfalfa before him which he was swallowing greedily. The Headman went forward and said: "Who brought him out?"

"No one has brought him out," Granny Khanoom said, "He's come out himself."

"How has he come out himself?" the Headman said, "We had tied his legs."

The women drew aside. Islam went forward and looked at the torn rope around the Redhead's leg, the knot that Mashdi Safar's son had knit was on his ankle like an anklet and the rest of the rope was gathered under his thigh like a coiled snake. Islam took the rope and pulled it. The Redhead turned and looked with full mouth. The Headman bent down and said: "How did you tear the rope?"

The Redhead said nothing. He swallowed all that was in his mouth and picked up two other carrots. "What shall we do to you?" the Headman said.

The Redhead said nothing. The men went and gathered in front of Islam's house.

"This didn't work either," Islam said, "Think of something else."

"No use in thinking of something else," Mashdi Safar's son said, "I told you the very first day, we should have had made short work of it then."

"You say we should kill him?" the Headman said.

"Not now," Mashdi Safar's son said, "No need to kill it now, it's better to take and leave it in the desert."

"It'll come back," Mashdi Baba said, "It'll come back way sooner than you and I."

"It can be solved easily," Mashdi Safar's son said, "We'll take and leave it around Seyedabad or Khatoonabad or Hazavan, hunger won't let it come back to Bayal. It'll have to go to one of those villages."

"Not a bad idea." Islam said.

"When shall we do it?" the Headman said.

"Right now, and we won't hesitate." Mashdi Safar's son said.

The men rose. The red rim of evening was hiding when some of them fetched the Redhead. And Islam fetched the cart. Abdullah and Mashdi Safar's son lifted the Redhead and put him in the cart and poured carrots and pieces of stale bread before him. Islam sat on the driver's seat and the other men got on, and they moved.

"Wish we had brought a lantern too." Islam said.

"No, darkness is better." Mashdi Safar's son said, "It's better that no one sees us."

"Don't they know this kid in the other villages?" Islam said.

"Even if they don't know it, it'll himself tell where it's from." Abdullah said.

"You think eating would give him a chance to talk?" The Headman said.

"It's a pity the Redhead has come to this," Islam said, "It's a good deal of pity, how useful he was to Bayal. You remember?"

"Yeah, it was like grown-ups." Ismail said.

"It's all over now," Mashdi Safar's son said, "Don't think about it. As if it hasn't existed at all; or it's died in the time of famine, and is gone."

"Everyone is a pity. Everyone's wasted." The Headman said. When they were in the desert nobody talked anymore. The moon, bruised and swollen, rose from the East. Two carts were moving toward Mishoo from Khatoonabad. Both carts were filled with potatoes and carrots and large packs. When they passed by the Bayalers the smell of toasted bread filled the entire desert.

## 7

The cart stopped on the by-way. Islam and the Headman and Mashdi Baba and Ismail and Mashdi Safar's son brought the Redhead down and took him into the darkness. Seyedabad was asleep. The Bayalers walked softly and reached the alfalfa field of Seyedabad. Islam emptied the full bag he had in his hand on the earth. The Redhead sat down and got busy with eating. The Bayalers went back on tiptoes. Islam sat on the driver's seat. The men got on softly and noiselessly. When they started moving, the sound of the Redhead's weeping filled the entire desert.

## 8

The Seyedabadians found the Redhead, who was sitting and swallowing the wheat stalks, in the stack; first they thought that a strange animal has come to the village. When they went closer they saw the Redhead with a rope that was knit to his leg, he was swallowing the stalks and moving ahead.

The Seyedabadians circled and watched.

"Where's it come from?" the First Seyedabadian said.

"It's not form Seyedabad, has it come from another village?" the second Seyedabadian said.

"Do you know it?" the first Seyedabadian said.

The Seyedabadians went closer and looked carefully. No one knew the Redhead; the first Seyedabadian sat down beside the Redhead who was eating ceaselessly with tired, lethargic eyes. The second Seyedabadian took the rope tied to his leg and pulled it. The Redhead's leg stretched and the Redhead said nothing.

"Where are you from?" the third Seyedabadian said.

"I'm hungry, I'm hungry." The Redhead said with his mouth full.

"Where have you come from?" the third Seyedabadian said.

"I'm hungry." The Redhead said.

The third Seyedabadian was angry and said: "What's your name? Which village are you from? Where have you come from?"

The Redhead said nothing, he filled his mouth and got busy with eating. The Seyedabadians looked at each other.

The sunshine was cast and the stack was shining like a river, and the Redhead was laying and he was filling his mouth quickly.

The first Seyedabadian said: "Someone must go and give news to the Beggar lady that something has come to the village which eats everything. What shall we do to it? And someone must go and bring bread and onions and a pot of porridge or pottage for it."

Two Seyedabadians went and came after several minutes. The first one with a bag of bread and onions which he emptied entirely before the Redhead, and the second said while panting: "The Beggar lady says don't let it in the village. Throw it out. It's a plague. Don't let it come to Seyedabad."

The Seyedabadians waited. As soon as the Redhead ate and finished the victuals they took his limbs and mounted him on a donkey and moved toward Hassanabad.

## 9

There was nothing for the Redhead in Hassanabad. The children had surrounded him and were looking at him with horror. The Redhead would creep on all fours, pulling the rope on the earth after him. The old women came and bent and looked at him. The Redhead's hair was shaggy; his eyes were swollen and drawn together. His limbs had changed shape and were altered. His fingers and toes couldn't be seen. He would eat anything he could get. The old women were giving alms of bread and onions. The Redhead would swallow all of them quickly.

When their Headman saw him he said: "But this isn't a human. Where has it come from? What is it called? Who's brought it to the village?"

The old women kneeled before the Redhead and implored: "come, come, for the sake of God and his Messenger go away from here. Go away from Hassanabad."

The Redhead was stretched over the earth like a frog. He was straining to open his eyes, and he couldn't. The men had come and lined behind him, they were planning how to catch and take him out of the village. Everyone was afraid of the Redhead. And the Redhead was opening and closing his mouth ceaselessly.

## 10

A strange creature had come to Bayal and broken into the stack. It was like no animal. Its muzzle was long like the muzzle of a mouse. Its ears were standing erectly like a cow's ears. But its limbs had no hooves. Its short, triangle tail was hanging, two short horns which were just newly sticking out form under the skin could be seen below the ears. When it strained, its eyelashes would open and its eyes, which like a frog's eyes looked upward, would appear from under the horns. Several pieces of rag were hanging from its limbs. It was sitting and eating wheat.

"What on earth is this that's come to Bayal?" Mashdi Baba said.

"As for me, I haven't ever seen such an animal." Mashdi Safar's son said.

"Can it be a hyena?" Ismail said.

"No," the Headman said, "I've seen hyenas two or three times, they were never like this."

"Isn't it our own Redhead that's come back to the village?" Mashdi Safar's son said.

The Headman and Mashdi Baba looked at him with shock. The Headman said: "No way, but the Redhead didn't look like that!"

"Yeah," Mashdi Baba said, "And his face had no whiskers."

"I don't know," Mashdi Safar's son said, "Whoever it be, we must make short work of it."

"As for me, I can't do it." The Headman said.

"Neither can I." Mashdi Baba said.

"I can." Mashdi Safar's son said.

And he went and brought a very big stone from behind the stacks. The Headman and Mashdi Baba turned their backs to Mashdi Safar's son and stared at the ruined mill, the broken door of which the blowing wind was banging. Mashdi Safar's son raised the stone. He put one foot on one side of the animal and put the other foot on the other side. He let the stone fall. The creature, without making a noise, stretched on the earth. A yellow, slimy blood came out of its mouth. The Headman and Mashdi Baba went to the other side of the stacks to dig a pit for the carcass.

## 11

They dragged the Redhead out of Mishoo. Three robust men threw him in a cart and another man poured an armful of grass and turnip peels before the Redhead.

The Redhead was stretched on the floor of the cart. His eyes couldn't be opened. The children were gathered, throwing stones. The Redhead turned with full mouth and closed its eyes and grumbled. The kids laughed and ran away.

When the cart started moving and came out of the village the sun set and it got dark. The Redhead, who hadn't opened his eyes for several days, didn't realize that the sun had set and it was dark. Day or night, it made no difference to the Redhead.

## 12

Mashdi Enayat's son who was returning from the desert saw that the Redhead, with full mouth, is creeping in the alfalfa and dragging himself toward Khatoonabad. He softly went closer and looked. He bent down and took the rope which was tied to the Redhead's leg and pulled it up. The Redhead lied down with his head on the earth. Mashdi Enayat's son ran hurriedly and entered the village. He returned with his father and Mir-Hamzeh and two other Khatoonabadians.

"There it is father, what do you think it is? Where has it come from?" Mashdi Enayat's son said.

Mir-Hamzeh bent down and said: "So it's not from Khatoonabad?"

Mashdi Enayat sat on the earth and opened the Redhead's eyes with his hand and looked.

"Do you know it Headman?" one of the Khatoonabadians said.

Mashdi Enayat bent down and looked again. The Redhead's heavy eyelids drew together.

"Yeah, yeah," Mashdi Enayat said, "I knew it. I've seen this youth before, in Bayal."

"Who has brought it here?" Mir-Hamzeh said.

Mashdi Enayat's son stared at the swollen limbs and the altered shape of the Redhead's body and said: "For sure they've beaten and thrown it out of Bayal themselves."

"I don't reckon the Bayalers would do such a thing." Mashdi Enayat said.

"All these talk aside, now what shall we do with it?" Mir-Hamzeh said, "When they haven't kept it themselves, we wouldn't let it be a burden on our shoulders."

"Let's take and drop it in Bayal." Mashdi Enayat's son said.

"No, it's a bad thing to do, and it is too bad too," Mashdi Enayat said, "After all, we've eaten salt with the Bayalers."

"So why don't they observe the sanctity of salt and bring this plague and leave it here?" Mashdi Enayat's son said.

"Ok, but that's not how it's done." Mashdi Enayat said, "Wait, at night we'll take and leave it around there."

"What shall we do with it till night?" Mashdi Enayat's son said.

"Let's take it to the square." Mir-Hamzeh said.

They took the Redhead to the square of Khatoonabad. The children found out and came. At first they looked at him with shock. When their fear was gone they came forward. Sattar said to Mashdi Enayat: "What a stomach it has! It eats anything it gets."

"That's why it's clear that it comes from Bayal." Mashdi Enayat said.

"Yeah, yeah, it's clear from where the hell it comes." Sattar said.

The children had surrounded the Redhead. They searched the garbage on the side of the square and held anything they found to him, the Redhead would take and swallow all of them quickly. The Khatoonabadian women looked at him in wonder and burst into laughter.

## 13

It was near noon when they found the Redhead behind the stacks near by the mill. His muzzle was stretched like a mouse's muzzle, the wool on his head and face was tangled. His limbs were swollen and dirty, it seemed that he had grown hooves. The anklets on his legs were mud-stained. He was straining to open his eyes and he couldn't. Some pieces of rag were hanging from his limbs.

Mashdi Safar's son found him first. He called the men. All of them came.

"What's up?" Mashdi Baba said.

"One of those things has come again." Mashdi Safar's son said.

"O Imam of our times, what do you want to do to it?" Mashdi Baba said.

"I'm going to bring a stone." Mashdi Safar's son said.

Islam bent down and looked and said: "No, it's the Redhead, our own Redhead."

When the Redhead heard Islam's voice it softly groaned: "I'm hungry, I'm hungry."

"Shouldn't I bring a stone?" Mashdi Safar's son said.

"What are you talking about? Do you want to kill a man?" Islam said.

"Poor wretch, how its looks have changed." Ismail said.

"These are his last days." Islam said.

"You want to say that we must leave our works and take care of this animal?" Mashdi Safar's son said.

"No, don't worry," Islam said, "I'll never let him stay in Bayal."

"You want us to take it to Seyedabad or some other village?" the Headman said.

"You just let him alone. I and Mashdi Ismail will take him to the city." Islam said.

"So what?" Mashdi Baba said.

"So that your minds will be in rest and peace!" Islam said.

And he sat down beside the Redhead, he opened his napkin and brought out two loaves of bread and put them before the Redhead. The Redhead opened its eyelids to look at Islam. His eyes were looking at somewhere else like a frog's eyes. The Redhead couldn't see Islam.

## 14

The Redhead was creeping on all fours in the main square of the city, moving forward and pulling the rope tied to his ankle after him. A large crowd had surrounded him; they were looking at him shocked; at the way he, with closed eyes, dragged himself on the ground and advanced. The children poured fruit peels and bread and waste paper and garbage before him and the Redhead swallowed all of them.

A tall, young man who was standing in the middle of the crowd said: "I saw it. I saw with my own eyes that it came out from the sewer. You know, from the same place where once two big creatures had been caught and they said they were beavers."

An old woman said: "What if it's come from the fairies?"

The man who was standing beside her said: "So, what do you say we shall do to it?"

The tall, young man said: "Let's call a cop to take it to the sewer again."

A fat, folded man came. He pushed the crowd aside and went forward; he bent when he was beside the Redhead. He had a large mouse trap in his hand and the carcasses of four thin mice with long withered tails were hanging from the four sockets of the trap and were waving. He pushed the buttons of the trap and the four mice, one after another, fell down before the Redhead.

# Eighth Story

## 1

Islam appeared from the little square behind Mashdi Safar's house driving the cart and came to the side of the pool. He got off and loosened the shafts and brought out the bucket from under the cart, he bent to fill it with water when Mashdi Baba's voice filled the air: "Hey, Mashdi Islam, hey Mashdi Islam!"

Islam turned around and saw Mashdi Baba who had put his head out of the hole over the door and was calling him. He put the bucket on the cart and looked at Mashdi Baba and put his hands around his mouth and cried: "Hey, hey Mashdi Baba!"

"Two men are looking for you." Mashdi Baba said from up there.

"For me?" Islam said.

"Yeah," Mashdi Baba said, "Two Seyedabadian youths. Haven't you seen them?"

"What did they want?" Islam said.

"Shah-Taghi has sent them for you," Mashdi Baba said, "When they saw that you're not here they went to the desert. Didn't you see them?"

And he took his head in. "What does Shah-Taghi want with me?" Islam said to himself.

And he returned to the cart, when Mashdi Safar's son appeared with the two young Seyedabadians from the second alley.

"Mashdi Islam is back, there he is." Mashdi Safar's son said.

The Seyedabadians came forward and Mashdi Safar's son also came and stood behind the Seyedabadians.

"These two have come for you from Seyedabad Mashdi Islam." Mashdi Safar's son said.

"Shah-Taghi has sent us." One of the Seyedabadians said.

"What does he want with me?" Islam said.

"Shah-Taghi asked you to pick up your instrument and come to Seyedabad with us." The second Seyedabadian said.

"What's up?" Islam said.

"It's his son's wedding," the first Seyedabadian said, "He asked you to come and play the instrument."

"What about my works?" Islam said.

"Forget about your works." Mashdi Safar's son said.

"When the wedding is finished you'll return to work." The second Seyedabadian said.

"How many days does it take?" Islam said.

"It takes no more than three days." The first Seyedabadian said, "Shah-Taghi has told us to be sure to take you there."

Islam thought and said: "Then, I'll call on the Headman and I'll be back."

Islam went to the second alley. The Seyedabadians went and sat on the black stone for washing the dead.

"The Headman's house is just around here," Mashdi Safar's son said, "He'll be back in no time."

"So we'll sit here till he comes back." The first Seyedabadian said.

"What about you? Don't you want to come?" the second Seyedabadian said to Mashdi Safar's son.

"Yeah, come, you'll have a whale of time." The first Seyedabadian said.

"Shah-Taghi won't be annoyed?" Mashdi Safar's son said.

"First of all, Shah-Taghi won't be annoyed," the first Seyedabadian said, "And, there are too many guests and he won't find out. Besides, Shah-Taghi's sight isn't good at night."

"Will you come?" the second Seyedabadian said.

"I'll come," Mashdi Safar's son said, "I'll go home and tell them and I'll be back."

And he went toward his house. When Islam returned a crowd had come and gathered around the cart.

"Let's go." Islam said.

"Wait till Mashdi Jafar comes too." The first Seyedabadian said.

"What's he going to do?" Islam said.

"It was agreed that he comes to the wedding." The second Seyedabadian said.

"So I'll go and bring my instrument." Islam said.

And he opened a path from between the crowd and went toward his house; he opened the window and entered. The black goat was sitting in front of the hatch in the store and looking out. When it saw Islam it rose and came forward. Islam took his instrument off the nail and came out by the window. The black goat also came out by the window. Both of them went and reached the cart.

"What a big instrument this Mashdi Islam has got!" the first Seyedabadian said.

"It just looks like a gendarme's rifle." Ismail said.

Islam laughed and said nothing. He hung his instrument on his shoulder and picked the bucket up from over the cart and hung it from the hook under the cart and said to Ismail: "Take the goat to your house till I come back."

Ismail went forward and grabbed the goat by the horns. Islam sat on the driver's seat and turned his face toward the Seyedabadians and Mashdi Safar's son who had come and sat beside the Seyedabadians, and said: "Ok now, get on to go."

"Won't you even let us light a pipe?" the first Seyedabadian said.

The second Seyedabadian laughed and said: "Mashdi Islam is much more in hurry than you and I."

He brought his tobacco bag out and gave it to Mashdi Safar's son who had brought his pipe out to light it. Islam got off the cart and went and sat on the edge of the pool and turned his back to the people and said: "Let me know when you're finished."

And he looked at his own image which was cast on the water, and the fingerboard of his instrument had stuck out from over the shoulder like a rifle.

Mashdi Safar's son winked. First the Seyedabadians laughed and then the crowd who were standing around the cart.

## 2

Islam was sitting on the driver's seat and whirling the whip around his head and coming closer to Seyedabad. The Seyedabadians were sitting beside Islam and Mashdi Safar's son had squatted in the middle of the cart and drawn up his knees to his belly. When Seyedabad appeared from a distant Islam's frowns disappeared and he turned and looked at the young men. The Seyedabadians who had thought that Islam was angry smiled broadly. Mashdi Safar's son turned and looked at the three men. The first Seyedabadian winked at Mashdi Safar's son.

"By the way," Islam said, "For which one of his sons has Shah-Taghi taken a wife?"

"But Shah-Taghi has no more than one son." The second Seyedabadian said.

"Yeah, you're right," Islam said, "By the way, what's his name?"

"They call him Mashdi Shafi." The second Seyedabadian said.

Mashdi Safar's son nodded and said: "Mashdi Shafi. Mashdi Shafi."

The Seyedabadians laughed. "Whose daughter has he married?" Islam said.

"Why do you want to know?" the second Seyedabadian said.

"He wants to know her." The first Seyedabadian said.

"You want to know her Mashdi Islam?" the second Seyedabadian said.

Islam shrugged and said: "I don't know."

The first Seyedabadian said: "Don't be annoyed Mashdi Islam, he's married uncle Zeinal's daughter."

"Which uncle Zeinal?" Islam said.

"The one who fell into a well and died last year." The first Seyedabadian said, "The girl lives with her aunt, Mashdi Roghayeh. That fatty woman. You know her, don't you?"

Mashdi Safar's son nodded and said: "Mashdi Roghayeh?"

"Mashdi Roghayeh herself has a lot of suitors, but she's not going to marry." The first Seyedabadian said.

"Hasn't she married yet?" Islam said.

"Why yeah. Her husband has died and she hasn't married again, and she has no children either." The second Seyedabadian said.

"Shah-Taghi can marry Mashdi Roghayeh himself." Mashdi Safar's son said.

"But Shah-Taghi has got his own wife and children." The first Seyedabadian said, "And besides, Mashdi Roghayeh isn't going to marry."

"For sure she wants a rich man to marry her." Mashdi Safar's son said.

"What does she want a rich husband for?" the first Seyedabadian said, "She's gone to the Beggar lady and sworn not to marry again."

"Why has she done so?" Mashdi Safar's son said.

"So that men would let her alone," the second Seyedabadian said, "She's got everything herself, a farm, cows, horses, a cart. What she wants a husband for?"

"But horses and cows cannot do a husband's job?" Mashdi Safar's son said.

The Seyedabadians laughed, Mashdi Safar's son started laughing too. Islam who was near Seyedabad stopped the cart and frowned and looked at the Seyedabadians and said: "Why do you laugh? Huh?"

The Seyedabadians and Mashdi Safar's son looked at each other, and when the Seyedabadians saw that Islam is angry, they stopped laughing.

"We weren't laughing at you Mashdi Islam." Mashdi Safar's son said, "We were laughing at Mashdi Roghayeh."

The Seyedabadians started laughing again.

## 3

Shah-Taghi's house was in the foremost part of the village and the other houses of Seyedabad were piled upon each other in the upper part. Shah-Taghi had gone on the roof and was sitting there and scaring the crows, which had come to ransack the wheat kernels, with his cane. Mashdi Shafi was cutting firewood in front of the door. He was wearing a green shirt and a yellow-colored vest. Mashdi Shafi's mother and four or five other old women had brought out a big, wooden chest from the store and were looking for something in the rags. The Seyedabadians were busy, coming and going on the roofs. The Beggar lady's house was empty, a small, black banner was waving gently upon the roof. The bride's house was several roofs higher. Three stables passed along Shah-Taghi's roof and reached uncle Zeinal's house, and upper, Mashdi Roghayeh's house around the roof of which was drawn a worn out palisade. Mashdi Roghayeh was sitting on the whetstone upon the roof and was clearing wheat and had hung her feet down into the store from the roof-hole. The bride was sitting in the store, she had taken apart a rosary and was sewing its beads on the fringe of her dress and every once in a minute she looked at the large shadow of the aunt's legs which was cast on the wall and had darkened the store. When the bride sewed the last rosary bead, the aunt pulled her legs out of the hole and cursed a crow that was hanging around her importunately. The crow flew and perched on the ledge of Shah-Taghi's roof and craned and stared at the stuff lying before Shah-Taghi. Shah-Taghi threw his cane at the crow. The stick fell in the chest in which Mashdi Shafi's mother and the old women were exploring.

"What's up?" Mashdi Shafi's mother said loudly.

Mashdi Shafi turned and looked. When Shah-Taghi rose, he saw Islam's cart and went forward hurriedly and bent down and cried: "They came. They brought Mashdi Islam."

He turned and looked at the bride's house and saw that Mashdi Roghayeh has come to the edge of the roof and has shaded her eyes with her hand and is joyfully and loudly crying with laughter: "They came. They came."

Mashdi Shafi put the axe behind the door and went to the kitchen. Mashdi Shafi's mother and the old women came to the front of the door and looked out. The Seyedabadians' and Mashdi Safar's son's laughter could be heard from far away.

## 4

When they finished eating Shah-Taghi called Islam. The two of them went out.

"Who's the one who has come with you?" Shah-Taghi said to Islam.

"He's Mashdi Safar's son." Islam said.

"Have you brought him here?" Shah-Taghi said.

"He's come himself, I haven't brought him." Islam said.

"He's not a good man," Shah-Taghi said, "I know him. He's got a habit of picking on everybody."

"Yeah, he's really wicked." Islam said.

Shah-Taghi thought and said: "You know Mashdi Islam, tonight is Mashdi Shafi's wedding. I want you to be in charge of everything in the wedding. I can't see clearly at night, I'm afraid it gets overcrowded or the guests aren't taken care of."

"You can be sure!" Islam said.

Shah-Taghi opened a low door and entered and signaled to Islam with his hand. The two of them climbed the stairs and reached a hatch which had been set on the ceiling. They opened the hatch; first Shah-Taghi pulled himself up and then Islam. They reached a large room which had small squared windows. Islam looked, there was a high wall in front of the window and a large nail was rammed into the heart of the wall and a short rope was tied to the nail. Shah-Taghi went to the upper end of the room and opened another low door, first himself and then Islam entered. It was a square room which had no windows, from the hole in the roof the light of evening was coming in. A large jar was put by the wall and a small ladder was leant against the jar's waist. There were also two large cans there. Shah-Taghi clapped on the jar and said: "You see it?"

Islam smiled. "Climb, and fill one of the cans." Shah-Taghi said.

Islam climbed up and opened the lid of the jar and Shah-Taghi gave him one of the cans.

When they came down, they put the tin can behind the door. Islam wiped his mouth, they came out. Shah-Taghi locked the door. Islam, whom a sweet giddiness had overcome, picked up his instrument and came to the large room with Shah-Taghi, the guests had come and filled every spot, and a large number were sitting on the verandas. The voice of women could be heard from the next room. Shah-Taghi drew the curtain. The women opened the door. Islam went to the upper end of the room staggeringly and sat on a large stool they had put for him and embraced the instrument's belly and put his hand on the strings and said: "To the merriment and long life of the bride and the groom."

Mashdi Safar's son and the two young Seyedabadians' laughing rose from the other corner of the room.

Islam, struck by surprise, listened to the laughs for some moments and suddenly brought down all his five fingers on the strings. When the sound of the instrument rose, the guests stirred and clapped and the wedding began.

## 5

Three other men sang as well as Islam. But nobody sang as good as Islam did. But every time Islam's voice rose, Mashdi Safar's son and the two young Seyedabadians' laugh filled the room.

At the night, the tumult of the guests increased. Islam and Mashdi Heidar, Mashdi Shafi's uncle, climbed the ladder several times and came down with the filled can. Shah-Taghi was sitting on the veranda and had hung his legs down and was laughing loudly and falling into fits unduly. The women had drawn the curtain aside and were coming and going among the men. After a while, Mashdi Shafi's mother opened a path for herself and came to Islam and said in his ear: "Now, it's time Mashdi Islam."

Islam went among the women after Mashdi Shafi's mother. Mashdi Shafi's mother loudly said to the crowd: "Get up and let's go bring the bride."

The crowed screamed with joy and Islam loudly said: "Merriment and long life."

And he started playing the instrument. Three old women came and stood beside Mashdi Shafi's mother. "Don't keep waiting, go to the yard." Mashdi Shafi's mother said.

"Why do you send them to the yard?" Islam said.

"We must go to the bride's house." Mashdi Shafi's mother said.

"I have nothing to do with the others. I'm going to the yard alone." Islam said.

He turned to go, he saw Mashdi Safar's son and the two young Seyedabadians who were watching him, and he didn't go to the room in which men were sitting, he went down by the wooden stairs before the window. Nobody was in the yard. A large wooden trunk was lying in front of the kitchen. Inside the kitchen was dark and three old women were standing in front of the fireplaces and were watching for the fire under the boilers. Islam sat on the trunk. The sky was full of stars; a green, turbid light had risen from the desert.

Mashdi Shafi's mother cried from within the room: "Hey Mashdi Islam! Hey Mashdi Islam!"

Islam rose from on the trunk and swept his fingers on the strings. When the sound of the instrument rose, the men from the stairs on the right and the women from the stairs on the left rushed into the Yard. The old women came out from the kitchen and Islam climbed the trunk. The rooms were empty,

Shah-Taghi who was sitting on the veranda alone by himself, loudly cried: "Hey Mashdi Islam! Hey Mashdi Islam!"

Islam with a loud voice said: "Hey Shah-Taghi! Hey Shah-Taghi!"

"Where are you son? Why are you out of breath?" Shah-Taghi said.

Mashdi Safar's son and the two young Seyedabadians laughed. Islam jumped down the trunk and yelled and played the instrument. The crowd started toward the alley while applauding.

## 6

When they brought the bride out of Mashdi Roghayeh's house, the tumult increased. The women were walking in the front and the men in the back. The bride was walking among several old women and several children were lighting the way with lanterns. Two men were visible among the women. Mashdi Shafi in groom's clothes and Islam, who was staggering and playing the instrument and singing, could be seen among the crowd of women. Between Mashdi Shafi and Islam, Mashdi Roghayeh was walking. The men were walking after the women with slow steps.

When the last person came out of Mashdi Roghayeh's house, an old neighbor woman closed the door and put a lock on it. When the house was dark, the light of the lamp in the stable increased. The mice gathered before the door of the kitchen and peeped, when the entire crowd was away, they rushed out and swarmed toward the stairs.

On the turn in the alley an old woman came and drew Mashdi Shafi to a corner and said: "You, come and go home. Who's told you to come out?"

"Everyone came and I came too." Mashdi Shafi said.

"You must come with a lamp to welcome the bride." The old woman said.

The old woman and Mashdi Shafi passed among the crowd and went down running.

When the groom went away Islam cut his singing. "Are you tired Mashdi Islam?" Mashdi Roghayeh said.

Islam hung his hands and said: "I'm tired, I'm awfully tired."

"You've been singing and playing alone all the time." Mashdi Roghayeh said.

Islam laughed and said: "Nobody wants to help me."

"And they don't even let you refresh." Mashdi Roghayeh said.

"It's all right, it's a wedding, it can't be helped." Islam said.

"It's all that Shah-Taghi's fault who didn't send for you two days earlier." Mashdi Roghayeh said.

"Well, it's all right." Islam said.

"How did you come here?" Mashdi Roghayeh said.

"We came by the cart." Islam said.

"Whose cart was it?" Mashdi Roghayeh said.

"Two youths had come after me, then we got on the cart and came."

"I'm talking about the cart. Whose cart was it?" Mashdi Roghayeh said.

"Bayal has no more than one cart and that's mine." Islam said.

"Is its horse yours too?" Mashdi Roghayeh said.

"Of course it is." Islam said.

"How many horses do you have?" Mashdi Roghayeh said.

"I have a horse, a cart and a goat." Islam said.

"What else do you have?" Mashdi Roghayeh said.

"I have a house too, behind the pool." Islam said, "And I have this too."

He showed his instrument. "I have a house too. A cart and three cows and two horses." Mashdi Roghayeh said.

Islam laughed and said: "Good."

"But one of my horses is sick and I'm afraid that it would die." Mashdi Roghayeh said.

"What's wrong with him?" Islam said.

The uproar of the crowd increased. "I don't know what's wrong with it." Mashdi Roghayeh said.

"He will surely get well." Islam said.

"No one in Seyedabad has found out what's wrong with it." Mashdi Roghayeh said.

"Forget about the Seyedabadians." Islam said.

"Some people have come and seen it. First Mashdi Reza came and didn't find out anything." Mashdi Roghayeh said, "Some others also came and burnt straws and rags in the middle of the stable and couldn't do anything."

"When a horse is sick you must fasten it to a cart and take it to the desert." Islam said.

"My horse's mouth is left open and blood is flowing out of its lips. And it can eat nothing but water." Mashdi Roghayeh said.

"Blood?" Islam said, "But, why does it bleed?"

"And you don't know what a blood it is!" Mashdi Roghayeh said, "It doesn't stop even for a minute. Can you do something to it?"

"Why not, of course I can." Islam said.

Mashdi Roghayeh entreatingly said: "When are you going to do it Mashdi Islam?"

"Anytime you want." Islam said.

"We're too busy now. Wait till we get some free time." Mashdi Roghayeh said.

She laughed and hit Islam gently on the arm and said: "We've reached the groom's house."

Islam embraced the instrument's belly and while striking on the strings hardly, started singing. The women's hubbub rose who were inclining into the pit before the door and Islam saw that Mashdi Shafi, panting and with cellular lamp in his hand, is coming toward the crowd from the bottom of the pit.

## 7

When the guests left, Islam and Mashdi Heidar, with a lantern in his hand, climbed the stairs and reached the hatch that was set in the middle of the ceiling. They opened the hatch and went up, it was totally dark behind the windows. Mashdi Heidar opened the hatch at the foot of the wall. Islam put his instrument at the foot of the wall and handed the can to Mashdi Heidar who was pulling himself out of the hatch and then went in himself. Mashdi Heidar put the lantern on the niche by the jar. Then he climbed, and picked the lid of the jar up and started filling the empty can with a bowl that was tied to the waist of the jar.

"No need to fill it Mashdi Heidar, nobody's drinking any more." Islam said.

"What do you mean by nobody drinks?" Mashdi Heidar said, "I drink, you drink and Shah-Taghi drinks too."

"They've taken Shah-Taghi to the neighbor's house, he's asleep now." Islam said.

"What about you?" Mashdi Heidar said, "You're not asleep, are you?"

"I and you will just drink here and go down." Islam said.

"We'll drink here and will take it down and drink there too." Mashdi Heidar said.

And he filled the bowl and gave it to Islam from on the ladder. Islam sat on the ground. "Give me the bowl." Mashdi Heidar said.

"Wait," Islam said, "I can't drink it at once. It's very cozy and comfortable here."

"You even roared your own head off." Mashdi Heidar said.

"Shah-Taghi himself had told me." Islam said, "I'll drink now and it will be all right."

And he quaffed the bowl and gave it back to Mashdi Heidar. And said: "Drink, drink and let's go down."

"I'll be staying here. I'll never go down." Mashdi Heidar said.

"But I'm going." Islam said.

"Yeah," Mashdi Heidar said, "You're very fond of hanging around among women, aren't you? Well, now, come and have a bowl up here, it's so sweet up here, you know?"

"You'll drop in there and drown." Islam said.

Mashdi Heidar laughed and said: "So much the better."

Islam said nothing and came down the stairs. The house had become empty and the relatives were scattered here and there. Mashdi Shafi's mother was sitting on the chest; she had squatted and was asleep.

Islam, who had his instrument under his arm, went to the yard by the wooden stairs before the window and sat on the trunk. When the sound of his instrument rose, the rooms and the lights danced before his eyes.

## 8

When the sound of Islam's instrument rose, Mashdi Roghayeh went down the stairs before the window and said to Islam: "Mashdi Islam."

"What?" Islam said.

"I was looking for you." Mashdi Roghayeh said.

"For me?" Islam said.

"Yeah, I searched everywhere." Mashdi Roghayeh said.

"But I'm here." Islam said.

"Yeah," Mashdi Roghayeh said, "I say, let's go and see my horse now."

"But it's night and it's dark now, nothing can be seen." Islam said.

"We'll take a lamp." Mashdi Roghayeh said, "Nobody's around now, tomorrow it will get crowded again and you'll forget about it."

Islam said nothing. He put his instrument beside the wooden trunk. Mashdi Roghayeh went and brought the lantern from the kitchen, they climbed the ladder and reached the roof.

"Why did we come here? Aren't we going to your house?" Islam said.

"No, come this way, leave it to me." Mashdi Roghayeh said.

They passed the roof of the stables and reached the roof of uncle Zeinal's house. Mashdi Roghayeh turned down the wick of the lantern and then jumped into an enclosure. Islam also jumped. Mashdi Roghayeh put the lantern by the wall and opened the hatch at the foot of the wall and a red light came out. Islam put his head in. it was a large stable with a lantern hanging on the pole. Three cows had their heads in the pen and an empty sack was nailed to the pole in the middle of the stable like a carcass. A thin horse was standing in the middle of the stable with its head hung down. Mashdi Roghayeh put her head in from the same hatch, she called the horse which came and stood before the two of them. Islam grabbed the horse's ears and pulled its head out. The horse's eyes were closed and a thick serum was flowing out of its half-open mouth.

"You see it?" Mashdi Roghayeh said.

Islam wiped the horse's tears with his hand and said: "Now, fetch a handful of dust."

Mashdi Roghayeh rose and went to the other corner of the roof and brought a handful of dust and poured it before Islam.

Islam took Mashdi Roghayeh's chuddar and wrapped it around his left hand and opened the horse's mouth and crammed his fist between the animal's jaws. Mashdi Roghayeh raised the lantern, the horse's dark throat lighted up, Islam picked the dust up with his right hand and sprinkled it into the horse's mouth. The horse closed its eyes and kept its mouth open as it was. Islam sprinkled another handful of dust into the dark cavity of the horse's throat and pulled his fist out. The horse moved backwards and coughed. The cows took their heads out of the pen and looked at the horse.

"What happened?" Mashdi Roghayeh said.

"It's all right now." Islam said, "Some leeches had stuck to his throat which are done for now. He won't spit blood anymore."

Mashdi Roghayeh closed the hatch. Islam unwrapped Mashdi Roghayeh's chuddar from around his left hand and threw it on the floor of the enclosure. As he rose, three shadows drew themselves back from over the wall and laughed boisterously.

Mashdi Roghayeh was scared and said with fear: "Who was that?"

"Mashdi Safar's son and the Seyedabadians." Islam said.

## 9

Islam bent down and put his head in from the roof-hole and softly said: "Mashdi Heidar?"

There was no answer. Islam again said: "Mashdi Heidar."

The light of the lantern had lighted the body of the jar and the stairs of the ladder.

"Why don't you answer Mashdi Heidar?" Islam said, "Have you gone down?"

Mashdi Heidar's voice was heard who said: "What do you want?"

And then he crept to the middle of the stairs. The lantern lighted his face.

"Do you see me?" Islam said.

"Don't you want to come in?" Mashdi Heidar said.

"I want to tell you something." Islam said.

"What do you want to tell me?" Mashdi Heidar said.

"I'm leaving tomorrow." Islam said, "I'm setting out tomorrow before the dawn."

"What's happened?" Mashdi Heidar said, "Has somebody said something? Has somebody annoyed you? Or are you tired?"

"I'm just going." Islam said.

"At least wait till I see what's happening." Mashdi Heidar said.

"Fill a bowl and send it up." Islam said.

Mashdi Heidar filled the bowl and slowly climbed the stairs of ladder. He put one foot on the orifice of the jar and hooked his left hand to the edge of the hole and sent the bowl up from the narrow orifice of the hole.

## 10

It was the blaze of the noon when Islam reached the pool. The village wasn't crowded and some pieces of cloud had cast shadow over the pool.

Islam got off the cart. He put his instrument on the cart and sat down on the black stone for washing the dead. Abbas's sister who was at the fountain went and called Ismail. Ismail came out with the black goat and went to Islam. Mashdi Safar put his head out of the roof-hole and looked out and saw that Islam is sitting on the black stone for washing the dead and is holding his head between his hands. "Hey, Mashdi Islam." Ismail said in a loud voice.

Islam turned around and looked. The black goat bit a little bush which had stuck out from under the black stone for washing the dead and swallowed it.

"You're back so soon Mashdi Islam!" Ismail said.
"What's going on in Bayal?" Islam said.
"Nothing." Ismail said.
"How's the Headman?" Islam said.
"Just the same as you saw him yesterday." Ismail said.
"Sit down and bring out your pipe." Islam said.

Ismail sat down. He brought out his tobacco bag and pipe. "Who's thrown these stones in the back of my house?" Islam said.

"I don't know." Ismail said.
"It must be a coward's work." Islam said.
"Which coward?" Ismail said.
"I know him." Islam said.

Islam said nothing, he looked at the houses and roofs of Bayal, and Mashdi Safar's head was visible like a pumpkin on the roof.

"Where are you looking at?" Ismail said.

Islam didn't answer and stretched his arm and took the pipe from Ismail's hand.

## 11

When Islam woke up, the sunshine was spread in the room from the little hole in the store. The black goat was by the widow, looking out. Islam sat up. He had slept with his cap and clothes on during the entire night.

The hubbub of women was coming from the pool. He rose and went and looked at the clearing behind the house from the hole in the store, and at his horse which he had tied to the withered trunk of a tree. The horse was in the shade and had brought its head down. A thick serum was flowing out of its mouth. "What if something's happened to him?" Islam said to himself, "Has he drunk water in Seyedabad?"

He took the enameled bowl and went to the room. He opened the window and came out. The women were busy all around the pool, washing dishes and clothes. When they saw Islam, their voices were cut and they rose and ran to the alleys. Islam looked at the women in a shocked manner and then came to the edge of the pool and bent down and looked at himself in the water and then filled the bowl with water and went to the back of the house. He rolled the stone door and entered the clearing; the horse turned and looked at him. Islam held the bowl before the horse's mouth. The horse didn't drink water.

Islam poured the water on the earth and threw the bowl beside the wall, he held the horse's head up and looked at its eyes. A man's shadow spread in the clearing and another man's soft voice from the neighboring roof said: "What's he doing?"

"He's standing beside the horse." The other voice answered.

And a third said: "Sure he's thinking about getting the cart and going to Seyedabad."

The second laughed and said: "So Mashdi Jafar is right."

Islam raised his head. Several pairs of eyes were looking at him from the hole in the neighbor's downpipe.

## 12

Islam was sitting behind the widow in darkness. A brim of moonlight was cast into the store. Papakh's sound could be heard from outside Bayal. Some people were walking beside the pool. Islam bent and looked. He saw Mashdi Baba and Ismail and Mashdi Safar's son who were walking ear to ear with each other and whispering and laughing.

## 13

Next day in the morning, Mashdi Baba came to Islam who was going to assemble the wheels of the cart.

"Mashdi Islam, I want to tell you something." Mashdi Baba said.

"What do you want to tell me?" Islam said.

"Do you know some gossip is spread in Bayal." Mashdi Baba said.

"What gossip is spread?" Islam said.

"That you wanted to take a wife in Seyedabad?" Mashdi Baba said.

"I didn't want to take a wife," Islam said, "Besides, would it be a sin if I had done so?"

"They say that they've seen you and Mashdi Roghayeh who were sleeping in each other's arms on one of the roofs." Mashdi Baba said.

"Who said?" Islam said.

"Last night they were gathered at the little square at the back of Mashdi Safar's house and Mashdi Safar's son had come and stood on the firewood and he was telling how he had come with the Seyedabadians and found you on the roof of the stable when you and Mashdi Roghayeh were in each other's arms." Mashdi Baba said.

"What did the Bayalers' say?" Islam said.

"They had believed it." Mashdi Baba said.

"What about you?" Islam said.

"I? I didn't believe." Mashdi Baba said.

"What did you say? What did you do to them?" Islam said.

"I said Mashdi Islam can never be accused of such labels." Mashdi Baba said.

"What else?" Islam said.

"And I told them I'll give a hard slap on the mouth to anybody who would talk behind Mashdi Islam's back." Mashdi Baba said.

Islam laughed and said nothing and got busy with the cart again.

## 14

About the evening, Mashdi Islam came back from the desert. The cart was filled with alfalfa and Islam was sitting on the alfalfa. When he was beside the Landlord's garden, he got off and unloaded the alfalfa. It was gradually getting dark when his work was finished.

Islam looked around him. The moon, swollen and gray, was visible from among the boughs. When Islam was going to get on the cart, a stranger riding a small cart appeared who came hurriedly and stopped and looked at Islam and said: "Won't you come to Seyedabad with me?"

Islam was horrified and said: "No, I won't."

"Where will you go then?" the stranger said.

"I'll go home." Islam said.

"Don't go home Mashdi Islam." The stranger said.

"Where shall I go then?" Islam said.

"You'd better get out of Bayal and go away," the stranger said, "You can't walk tall in Bayal anymore."

"Where are you coming from?" Islam said.

"I was passing by here. I had no business in Bayal." The stranger said.

And he raised his whip and moved. Islam stood and looked at him. The stranger went away and disappeared in the darkness. The sound of a bell could somehow be heard from far away.

Islam left the cart behind the Landlord's garden and entered the village and went toward the little square at the back of Mashdi Safar's house.

The men were sitting around and Mashdi Baba was sitting on the firewood and talking quickly and the Bayalers were listening. A small lantern was burning over Mashdi Baba's head. Islam drew himself to the side of the wall and stood there. Mashdi Baba said: "Then they go up with Mashdi Heidar and when they come down Islam can't get his feet on the earth anymore."

Mashdi Safar's son rose from behind the firewood, who said: "Mashdi Heidar doesn't come down, he stays up there and Islam comes down alone."

"Yeah," Mashdi Baba said, "He comes down alone and searches everywhere to find Mashdi Roghayeh and he can't. He goes and sits on the wooden trunk and plays the instrument, and then Mashdi Roghayeh goes to him. The two of them rise and go on the roof. And the Seyedabadians after them, and at last they find them when on the roof of the stable…, oh, yeah, Mashdi Roghayeh's chuddar was thrown in a corner and the rest is clear. The Seyedabadians consider Bayal's reputation and return quietly. Two hours later Islam appears, who comes and hangs from the ladder and falls on the earth from up there…"

Islam turned and came to the alley. Mashdi Baba's voice could be heard from a distance who was loudly saying: "He remains on the earth till the morning and when they go to him they see that he's thrown up and the ladder has fallen on his breast and they think that…"

Islam went away with long steps and heard no more.

## 15

In the morning, before the dawn, Islam took his instrument and came out with the black goat. He put the instrument by the black stone for washing the dead and went toward the Headman's house. He jumped into the yard from over the wall. He took the shovel and the pickaxe and came out. He went and dug the earth in front of his house. When the dust was ready, he brought water and made mud and went and opened the widow and looked inside the room. He took off his shoes and threw them in the middle of the room on the wheels and parts of the cart which he had taken into pieces and had piled on each other last night. The room was dark. He had already covered the hatch in the store and the roof-holes at night. When he watched his room a good while, he closed the window and started mudding.

When the sun rose, the Bayalers came out and gathered around the pool and watched Islam who had put on mourning clothes and was working, pouring out sweat; when Mashdi Baba saw Islam he turned and looked for Ismail and said: "Run to the Headman and tell him to get himself to Islam's house at once."

"But the Headman is sick." Ismail said.

"I know, tell him to come," Mashdi Baba said, "Mashdi Islam is going to leave Bayal."

"Is he really going to leave?" Ismail said.

He turned and ran toward the Headman's house. "Hey, Mashdi Islam!" Mashdi Baba said in a loud voice.

Islam turned around and looked and said nothing.

Mashdi Baba called him again: "Hey, hey, Mashdi Islam, hey."

Baba Ali, who had put his head out of the hatch of the enclosure, said: "What are you doing Mashdi Islam?"

"Mashdi Islam is mudding his house." Granny Khanoom said to the women.

"Hey, Mashdi Islam!" Mashdi Baba said, "Why are you mudding your house?"

"I like to mud my house." Islam said.

"But, has something happened?" Mashdi Baba said.

"Nothing has happened." Islam said.

"Why do you do that?" Mashdi Baba said. "Do you want to go somewhere?"

"The house is mine." Islam said, "I do anything I like and go anywhere I like."

"But, has something happened?" Mashdi Baba said, "Has anybody said anything?"

Islam didn't answer. He finished his work and came down. He had mudded every hole and hatch. The house had become like a dome which had grown and come up from the flat earth. And he went and brought the horse out from the clearing at the back of the house and let it loose beside the pool. The black goat that was standing and looking at the crowd went toward the horse. And Islam went beside the black stone for washing the dead and took his instrument and hung it on his shoulder, when the Headman appeared with crutches under his arms. The Headman's face was swollen and he was dragging his swollen feet on earth with trouble.

"I would come to see you Headman. Why did you come out?" Islam said.

The Headman was shocked: "Do you want to go somewhere Mashdi Islam?"

"For me, it's time to leave. I can't stay in Bayal anymore." Islam said.

"You shouldn't leave Mashdi Islam." The Headman said, "These are my last days, I'm sure to go today or tomorrow. Don't you want to take care of my funeral?"

"As for me, I don't like to leave." Islam said, "But something's happened that I have to go away."

"What's happened?" The Headman said, "Has anybody done anything? If so, who's done it?"

The Bayalers who were standing all around the Headman didn't answer.

"Mashdi Islam," The Headman said, "If you leave there'll be nobody who can do a thing in Bayal. Why do you want to go away?"

"Ask them," Islam said, "Ask Mashdi Baba about all of it when I'm gone."

The Bayalers said in a chorus: "Don't go away Mashdi Islam. Don't go away."

"Don't go away?" Islam said, "I should stay to see your faces everyday? To hear your talk? Have you forgotten about yesterday?"

The Headman wept and said: "But what's happened? Why don't you tell me anything?"

Islam went and embraced the Headman and kissed his forehead and turned around, he went toward the crowd without saying anything. The crowd drew aside. Islam started walking toward the road. The crowd looked at him. The Headman sat down on the dust, and with a gloomy voice, said: "What have you done to him? What have you done to him? What disaster have you brought on him?"

And he cried bitterly. Mashdi Baba said: "I don't know. I don't know anything."

Papakh and Islam's black goat appeared from the little square at the back of Mashdi Safar's house and came and passed between the crowd and followed Islam several steps and then stood and watched Islam. And the horse with its head hung down went beside the willow. It looked at the earth with half-closed eyes, brought out its large, parched tongue and started licking the black stone for washing the dead; from the corners of its lips, pieces of clotted blood were flowing out.

## 16

Three days later, around the evening, when the sky was cloudy and gloomy, Islam had embraced his instrument's belly and was walking on the sidewalks of the city; he was playing the instrument and singing. The crowds which were coming from the opposite side would draw aside and stop and watch the old rustic with his black shirt and strange instrument. They would hear his song, laugh and throw money for him.

Islam was wandering form one street to another and drawing a number of people after him.

Mashdi Islam was playing the instrument and the children laughed and the grown ups looked at him with surprise.

## 17

From far away, the sound of a lonely instrument was coming and the sound of the laughing of a crowd who were gradually coming closer. Behind the bars of the hospital, the sick were gathered and were peeping to see the player of the instrument. The familiar song was getting closer. And the tall pines of the hospital were standing motionlessly.

## 18

Three days later, around the evening, when the sky was cloudy and it was gloomy and it was damp, Mashdi Roghayeh and Mashdi Heidar and the two young Seyedabadians came to Bayal with two horses. Mashdi Baba who had put his head out of the hole over the door saw them who came and stood beside the pool. No one was in sight in the village. Islam's black goat was sitting in front of the mudded window and was dozing off.

"Hey, hey, Seyedabadians, who are you looking for?" Mashdi Baba said in a loud voice.

The Seyedabadians looked and didn't see Mashdi Baba. Mashdi Baba put his cap on his head and came out. Several men and women of Bayal also came out and gathered around the newcomers. The horses went to the edge of the pool and hung their heads into the pool. Mashdi Safar's son came and the Seyedabadians called him.

"What have you come for?" Mashdi Safar's son said.

"We've come to see Mashdi Islam." The first Seyedabadian said.

"What do you want with him?" Mashdi Safar's son said.

"We want with him." The second Seyedabadian said.

Mashdi Safar's son nodded his head at Mashdi Roghayeh, winked and softly said: "She wants with him?"

Mashdi Roghayeh turned around and looked at him angrily and said: "Yeah, I want with him, is it your business?"

Mashdi Baba, who found out whom they had come to see, said: "Mashdi Islam's gone to the city."

"He's gone to the city?" Mashdi Heidar said, "When will he come back?"

"It's not clear when he comes back." Mashdi Baba said, "And maybe he won't come back, God knows."

"Hasn't he told you when he will return?" Mashdi Roghayeh said.

"I don't know, and nobody knows either." Mashdi Baba said, "There, it's his house which he has mudded and he's gone away."

"What shall we do?" Mashdi Roghayeh said to Mashdi Heidar.

Both of them turned around, they looked at Islam's house and Islam's black goat.

"Has something happened?" Mashdi Baba said.

Mashdi Heidar didn't answer. Mashdi Roghayeh said: "What shall we do?"

"Has something happened?" Mashdi Baba said to the young men.

The young men shrugged and said nothing. Mashdi Roghayeh went to the horses and put her hand on one of the horses' back and loudly said: "I don't know what to do to them."

She turned and looked at Islam's house again. Mashdi Baba and Mashdi Safar's son went closer and looked at the horses which were standing with their legs parted and had hung their heads into the pool. The mouths of both of them were half-open and purple-colored clots of blood were bubbling from their throats and foaming and coming out and flowing into the pool, one piece after another, and coming alive, like tiny and large frogs, which having been rescued from a dark, narrow sewer, had reached a slime-filled pool.

www.ingramcontent.com/pod-product-compliance
Lightning Source LLC
Chambersburg PA
CBHW032252150426
43195CB00008BA/424